THE
ADMINISTRATION
OF
INJUSTICE

*the text of this book is printed
on 100% recycled paper*

THE
ADMINISTRATION
OF
INJUSTICE

MELVIN P. SIKES
The University of Texas at Austin

Harper & Row, Publishers
New York, Evanston, San Francisco, London

Cover photo and Parts Two and Three photos by Michel Cosson.

Sponsoring Editor: Alvin A. Abbott
Project Editor: Holly Detgen
Designer: Michel Craig
Production Supervisor: Will C. Jomarrón

THE ADMINISTRATION OF INJUSTICE

Library of Congress Cataloging in Publication Data
Sikes, Melvin P.
         The administration of injustice.

         Bibliography: p.
         Includes index.
         1. Criminal justice, Administration of—United
States. 2. Police—United States. I. Title.
KF9223.S53   364   74-26683
ISBN 0-06-046146-2

*Dedicated to my wife, Zeta, who at my request helped me
to become strong so that she might safely lean on me.*

CONTENTS

PREFACE

Few subjects are more emotion laden than those dealing with the administration of justice. Whether discoursing on statutes or on the overworked issue of law and order, people tend to choose sides and to stoutly defend a position without regard to its actual defensibility. They seem to say, "Don't bother me with the facts! Can't you see, I'm defending a position!" This kind of response polarizes groups and may be one of the most potent, exacerbating factors in the sporadic acts of violence on the the part of some police and the more activist elements of our communities.

The deteriorating relations between police and various segments of our society have caused considerable emphasis to be placed on the need for improved police–community relations. However, this is only one aspect of the overall problem; and, although it deserves top priority, other elements of our criminal justice system must not be ignored.

More than passing acknowledgment must be accorded the facts related to discriminatory jail sentences, questionable bail bond procedures, unfair jury selection, discriminatory representation by counsel, conditions is overcrowded jails and prisons, crowded court dockets resulting from too few courts, and almost nonexistent appropriate screening, selection, and training of jail and prison personnel. The ethics of the judiciary as well as counsel might well be questioned in many instances—to say nothing of the ignoring of constitutional law by some local law authorities and the intrusion of personal bias both in judgment and in sentencing by some officials.

Our criminal justice system suffers more from an unconcerned, apathetic, or ignorant citizenry than from any combination of overt criminal acts. Justice is as much the responsibility of John Q. Public as it is the responsibility of those persons directly a part of the criminal justice system. It is a two-way street.

It is hoped that this material will prove beneficial in the continuing effort to develop optimum police–community relations and will generate active, positive interest in our beleaguered system of justice. Only by the acceptance of truth (no matter how bitter) and a willingness of all concerned to do whatever is necessary (no matter how difficult) will this major social problem be solved.

Further, it is hoped that this book will be an invaluable

source of information for the many dedicated law enforcement persons and others in the criminal justice system who represent the professional ideal. If this work helps the reader to understand the roots of minority group hatred for all law enforcement and if it helps the minority group individual to understand the weaknesses in our system of justice, together we may be able to build toward a better, safer society. Democracy may indeed be an attainable goal.

No country can grow and develop where there is no order, and a society without equal *justice will self-destruct. There* must *be law and that law* must *be tempered by justice. And that justice must be for all!*

The contributions of many individuals made this work possible. Endeavors to list the names of these many persons were abandoned because of a fear that some contributor might be overlooked. In a less efficient manner, but a more comprehensive one, I offer my deep appreciation to those individuals from the Community Relations Service of the U.S. Department of justice, police professionals from academies and other institutions designed both to train and to educate police officers, chiefs of police from a number of police departments, individual officers, and the several behavioral scientists who shared their experiences with me.

I am especially indebted to my research assistant, Warren Gibbs, whose dedication and talent greatly facilitated the accomplishment of this work.

In addition, I offer my profound gratitude to my secretary, Marcie Pickhardt, for her patience, her technical assistance, and her sacrificial support throughout the preparation of this book.

Finally, I want to thank Dr. Wayne Holtzman, President of the Hogg Foundation for Mental Health, The University of Texas at Austin, for his unstinted assistance.

MELVIN P. SIKES

THE
ADMINISTRATION
OF
INJUSTICE

INTRODUCTION

Historically, the police officer has not been a champion of the poor or of minority groups—particularly blacks, Mexican-Americans, and American Indians. Traditionally his role has been seen as that of policing minority groups and protecting white America. A general consensus of minority opinion in the recent past was that north of the Mason-Dixon line the police officer was concerned largely with organized crime, while in the South it was his responsibility to "keep the nigger in his place." The methods used by the "peace officer" were never questioned. Those who acted as judge, jury, and executioner were more often lauded for saving the sovereign state's money. Sadistic police practices against blacks were an accepted way of life for southern law enforcement officers, and generally were ignored by the white public, in the eyes of blacks. Such practices were convenient for thwarting the emergence of black manhood and for putting the fear of God in the hearts of those who would seek equal justice under the law for blacks and other minorities. There is sufficient historical and research evidence to give credibility to many of the attitudes and beliefs held by nonwhite minority groups in America.

Today these roles have been altered—much to the frustration and open resentment of many police officers over the country. The intent and the spirit of civil rights laws implied an immediate about-face in both prejudicial attitude and long-established discriminatory behavior. The determination of large numbers of law enforcement groups to resist obeying the law of the land had not been mitigated before a new and strange adjustment was demanded. The emergence of the so-called social revolution and the eruption of student protest and rebellion presented additional problems for the already overburdened police officer. Proficiently trained as he may have been in dealing with traditional criminal activity, he found himself totally unprepared psychologically or methodologically to handle social activism. In the language of modern youth, "It blew his mind." Unfortunately many law enforcement officials refused to admit their incapacity to cope with this dilemma until almost irreparable damage had been done. The result was hopeless frustration or vitriolic rage on the part of many officers. Their intense anger was manifested by increasing incidents of police brutality and a closing of police ranks at a national level. To citizens who were aware of the widening gap between law enforcement and minority groups and the young, the situation seemed both serious and dangerous.

LAW AND ORDER

The issue of law and order has forboding connotations for Afro-Americans and Mexican-Americans as well as for the poor of this country. For them it portends ultraconservative national trends and repressive police tactics. Many persons who wanted to believe in the positive intent of this concept feared rather that in practice a pervasive erosion of human rights might obtain and a police state might emerge. In that event, it was felt that no federal, state, or local agency and no public official would be in a position to clarify the meaning in the desired direction (that of reducing actual crime in the nation as opposed to a focus on suppressing even nonviolent dissent and civil rights thrusts). It was felt that all avenues to the protection of human rights would be closed while the individual, sadistic police officer enjoyed "open season" on blacks, Mexican-Americans, liberal whites, and any other groups that may have been resistant to an antebellum status quo. Denial of this possibility certainly seemed totally inconsistent with recent history.

What appeared to be an appalling inconsistency in the situation was the screaming for law and order among white Southerners who were mute in the days of open, unpunished lynching. No cry was heard during the bombings and killings in the nonviolent phase of civil rights activities. In fact, law enforcement officers were among the leaders in the wanton murders of those days. Not even when innocent little girls died in a church bombing in Alabama was there a demand for law and order. Research has shown a great migration of Ku Klux Klan-like members of police forces to the West, Midwest, and North, and their influence is obvious. They make the Omnibus Crime Bill an "Ominous" Crime Bill in the minds of many persons who support the spirit of this measure. Requests for money to be used for riot weaponry and chemicals greatly exceeded proposals that put their stress on training, research, and more sophisticated and efficacious ways of quickly detecting and apprehending criminals. Little concern was shown for an improved judiciary procedure and more efficient penal institutions.

To large numbers of persons the trend seemed to be toward suppression of individual rights, despite the American ideal as expressed by the fathers of our country. Jefferson was concerned about the rights of the minority. While giving attention to the importance of majority rule, in his Inaugural Address he was careful to point up the rights of the minority that must be given equal consideration:

> All, too, will bear in mind the sacred principle, that though
> the will of the majority is in all cases to prevail, that will
> to be rightful must be reasonable; that the minority possess
> their equal rights, which equal law must protect, and to vio-
> late would be oppression.[1]

History focuses upon majority rule to the exclusion of the minority question. Lincoln's statement regarding the citizens' right to dissent (First Inaugural Address, March 4, 1861) would have made him a prime target for ultraconservative organizations today. He declared:

> This country, with its institutions, belongs to the people who
> inhabit it. Whenever they shall grow tired of the existing
> government, they can exercise their constitutional right of
> amending it, or their revolutionary right to dismember or
> overthrow it.[2]

Though disenchanted, the average black man wants to love the only country he knows, the United States. Suggestions that he would attempt to overthrow the government are seen by him as ridiculous and intended only to mislead or further inflame those who seek to deny him the inalienable rights guaranteed by our Constitution.

SOME PSYCHOLOGICAL DIMENSIONS

Defensiveness and a kind of paranoia seem to characterize police behavior. Although many officers deny or justify the charge of being defensive, they admit their extreme suspicion of everyone—including family and friends. Some say this is learned behavior and is one of the hazards of the job. It appears to have played a major role in the high divorce rate among law enforcement officers. Some speculate that the defensiveness is a result of collective guilt.

Feelings of isolation from self and others, rejection by society, and a pervasive loneliness form a good psychological seedbed for depressive reactions. Clannishness and the creation of a closed society are manifestations of alienation. It should be obvious to law enforcement officials that the kinds of experiences to which police are constantly exposed can do psychological damage. Unfortunately, most law enforcement agencies deny a need for continuous mental hygiene support or ignore possible mental illness in the ranks of men whose responsibility entails protecting others, possibly at the cost of their lives.

Now a new element enters. The felt omnipotence of some officers is being challenged by various groups. Students and others know how to challenge the mental stability of the apparently most well-adjusted officer without doing him physical violence. On the other hand, the officer may face impotent violence from the young and the angry without being equipped to handle it efficiently. Rage, physical attack, and other violent means of reprisal often are the only weapons in his mental arsenal. He can only react, not act wisely. Sadly, for many, violence affords a perfect release for covert sadism, bigotry, or perhaps some type of latent mental illness that is triggered by psychological stress but goes quickly into remission when the pressure is removed.

Perhaps in a more enlightened day top police administrators will employ full-time or part-time mental health persons and group therapy will be an accepted, normal activity for all law enforcement agencies. Preventive mental health measures do not imply latent mental problems any more than protective medicine implies latent disease. Rather, the idea is to provide an immunizing agent against constant exposure to the dangerous psychological impact of an extremely demanding occupation.

THE RECRUITMENT QUESTION

Recruitment, a national problem, remains difficult. Poor image, poor pay, and poor working conditions are among the factors contributing to a lack of enthusiasm for police work. Few men have the courage or fortitude to join an embattled cause, especially if there seems to be no desire or intent to change on the part of those involved.

Effective law enforcement is crucial. It requires the best in intellect, integrity, objectivity, and emotional stability. Unfortunately, it also attracts sadists, psychopaths, bigots, and the like, many of whom pass poor screening tests and often rise to positions of high rank. Where there are no screening tests (a recent report indicated that few southern states administer psychological tests as a part of the screening process), the dangers of getting undesirables on the force are great; and once they are accepted it is almost impossible to remove them. Even psychological evaluation has not proved to be a panacea.

Few professions (if any) as important as law enforcement lack some national uniform standards of excellence. There appear to be *no* national norms for this group; and local standards vary from totally subjective appraisal to sophisticated screening techniques, so that police officers range from semi-illiterates to college graduates. Small towns tend to suffer most. Until standards are raised and until a degree of uniformity in selection and training is determined, the general public can be in as much danger from the unprofessional police officer as from the traditional criminal.

PUBLIC UNINVOLVEMENT

Until unlawful police practices are reviewed by other than police or law enforcement types, fair and impartial trial of accused officers will remain questionable. It should not be expected that police groups or policemen as a group are different from other close-knit groups. Each defends his own; and the human element precludes cold objectivity, particularly among persons whose very lives depend one upon the other. Maybe this again is a manifestation of our determination to make the police officer superhuman and our expectations that he can live up to the omnipotence we impose upon him.

The police officer is the most obvious symbol of the criminal justice system. First, he has the most contact with the general public. In addition, usually it is through his direct action that individuals are apprehended, tried, and possibly convicted. Unfortunately, he is seen more as the big, bad wolf than as the peace officer.

The public is generally aware of the fact that persons are apprehended, told their rights, arraigned, tried by a jury, and on the basis of conclusive evidence sentenced. (Although this is not always the case, theoretically this is how the procedure operates.) Few persons know or are concerned about bail bond procedures, the overall trial process, the jury system, the jails and prisons, the parole procedure, or other facets of the criminal justice system.

An apathetic and ignorant public has permitted continuous erosion of a vital system and continues to go blindly along, being aroused only when taxed or when fleetingly frightened by some announcement of the growing crime rate. Unless Americans become honestly involved, we *shall* wake up in a police state, or, at worst, our highly touted society will crumble under the burden of its own insensitivity.

PART ONE

TOWARD A
SYSTEM OF
INJUSTICE

INTRODUCTION TO PART ONE

Law enforcement agencies are a very important part of the criminal justice system. The upheavals of the middle 1960s seemed to bring into focus the hazy and suspect relationship between minority groups and law enforcement officers. Open conflict between police and so-called militant blacks was followed by violent confrontations between police and so-called left-wing white radicals. Charges and countercharges made obvious the fact that the image of the friendly police officer had changed to that of "pig."

Various types of police–community relations programs sought to bridge the communication gaps between police and the more activist elements of the minority and youth groups. These programs, along with stringent and repressive measures, put out the fires; but it was and is obvious that live coals lie smoldering. Only the naive believe that suppression is a solution; it treats only the symptom.

There are reasons for the problems faced by law enforcement agencies. Blacks, Mexican-Americans, and the poor are not innately hostile to police authority. Not all police are bigots and "pigs." Endeavors to improve relations between various segments of the community and the police are succeeding slowly but not always with basic understanding or mutual trust. There are still complaints of overreaction, brutality, discourtesy, harassment, and the like, by police officers. Citizens still seek recourse and often find none when they file complaints against law enforcement officers.

Difficulty in recruiting minorities continues to plague departments. The reasons are ignored or not faced in a forthright manner. Sometimes it results from a distrustful minority.

Problems to be solved must be accepted as problems, analyzed, and studied. Part One seeks to shed light on possible causes and offers some plausible approaches to solutions. Best solutions will come from persons involved and through their acceptance, understanding, and conscientious efforts to bring about a society that provides equal protection under the law for *all* of its citizens.

Part One is not without emotional impact because the problem itself is an emotional one for minorities. So strong are the feelings that the average officer would be "turned off" or overwhelmed were they openly expressed. However, to provide a realistic grasp of the degree to which minorities hate or the depth of their distrust or despair, it is mandatory that some of the emotion show itself in the writing. Otherwise (to accommodate sensitivity), the truth would be violated and the impact would be insufficient to help the officer "feel" with the black, the brown, the red, and the poor. The intent is to help the individual to walk a mile in the shoes of minority group persons as most of them view law enforcement. A heightened awareness should allow the individual officer to become more competent and will greatly facilitate his work as a peace officer.

CHAPTER 1

UNEQUAL PROTECTION
OF MINORITIES

The nigger has no rights that
the white man must respect.

This unwritten law of the Old South is still emblazoned on the hearts of many white Americans. It epitomizes an attitude that is insidious in nature and can be found among the most "liberal" elements of society. Since it has always been a part of the fabric of American life, its reinforcement, both consciously and unconsciously, by white American parents perpetuates the mental aberration and gives it credence.

A practical example comes from a graduate student ex-police officer and ex-teacher who wrote a paper on how he became a "bigot" despite "wonderful" liberal parents. During a trip through the Ford plant in Detroit, his mother accounted for the large number of blacks working in the foundry section by saying, "Their African ancestry suits them to greater heat tolerance."

She added to his "tolerance" by permitting him to play with "anyone we pleased, even Howard, my Negro friend." She suggested that Howard might like bright-colored and rhythmic things and that it was good his people belonged to the African Methodist Episcopal Church where they could worship "in their own ways with their own people and not be bothered by our ways."

The student's father indicated that Howard's father would work for less (as a janitor in the white church) than he would;

therefore Howard's father posed an economic threat to the student's family.

Opposition to interracial dating was based not on bigotry but on the possibility of interracial marriage and the ostracizing of children of such a union.

Finally, opposition to blacks buying homes in the neighborhood was not on racial grounds but on the fact that home values would go down and the student's father would lose a great deal of money.

This typically American "liberalism" illustrates only a few of the racial stereotypes that dehumanize minorities, brainwash whites, and indoctrinate the credulous. It follows that unequal people do not warrant equal protection. Schools, churches, courts, and other public and private organizations and agencies tend more to validate than to invalidate this un-American way of thinking.

The denial of human rights to the Negro—or black American—has its roots in the history of the slave period. Although the slave was ostensibly freed, the mind of his former master remained enslaved, particularly to his need to dominate. The causes of the need of the white American to dominate—in a viciously cruel manner—remain fertile ground for research. So urgent was this need during the slave period that when "Christian conscience" could no longer abide human bondage, a legal, constitutional move made Negroes chattel, thus relieving the conscience while permitting the maintenance of slavery.

Too, it legalized brutal physical attacks upon the bodies of men, women, and children (slaves) without need for compunction. Since slaves were no longer human (legally), buying, selling, and otherwise breaking up families, or mating with slave women, or mating "healthy males and females," or keeping certain males and females for "breeding purposes" was neither a sin nor illegal.

The Emancipation Proclamation, carefully worded to avoid disturbing the sensitivities of former slave owners or other white Americans, was designed more to discourage English intervention in the American Civil War than to encourage black liberation in America. This document legally freed a dehumanized, frightened, threatened, and defenseless mass of humanity. Many had no place to go and found themselves with no protection against a strange and hostile environment and without the most meager means of surviving. Large numbers did not survive.

In addition, freedom for the slaves was little more than a meaningless concept. It was made clear to the freedman that he was not recognized as a citizen. Only eight years later the Supreme Court declared unconstitutional the Civil Rights Act of 1875, which assured equal rights under the law. Of course, the act carried no enforcement provision, but it was at least a gesture toward truly democratic and fair govenment. White Americans in their malicious treatment of freed Negroes made no distinction between graduates of Harvard and recent graduates from the cotton fields. It was open season on blacks and they found themselves totally unprotected by responsible agencies.

The treatment of slaves and of freed or free Negroes was a missing segment in our earlier history books. Recent publications deal with the subject rather openly; and although this franker practice points to another embarrassing period in our history, it permits self-inventory and an opportunity to correct some past ills. In addition, it explains much of black attitude and feeling today, putting black history in a more correct perspective.

Protection is seen as a primary responsibility of law enforcement. The law enforcement officer swears to "defend the Constitution; to protect the innocent; to enforce the law courteously and equally," and the like. Although words may differ, the sense of every oath of office is impartiality in the enforcement of laws and, ultimately, in the administration of justice.

However, the black American has not been accorded impartiality in treatment by our system of justice. It is an accepted fact that historically laws have sought to protect white society by enslaving the black. Initially, they were meant to protect the white slaveholders. Later, they were to safeguard those "free, white, and twenty-one" from any social, economic, or educational challenge by freed blacks.

In such a context, the major role of the police officer was that of "keeping the nigger in his place." If the color of the "nigger" was brown in South Texas or red in New Mexico, the job of the enforcement agent was the same as in the Deep South where the "nigger" was black. In fact, history affords indisputable evidence of police neglect and/or police involvement in crimes against minorities.

An example of early police involvement in atrocities against Negroes occurred in New Orleans shortly after the Civil War ended. Civilians and police used stones, bricks, and clubs to rout Negroes who were proceeding peacefully to an assembly hall to discuss the franchise. The mob killed some immediately and pursued others, who were attempting to escape, and killed them. General Sheridan said of this:

> At least nine-tenths of the casualties were perpetrated by
> the police and citizens by stabbing and smashing in the heads

of many who had already been wounded or killed by policemen. . . . It was not just a riot but an absolute massacre
by the police . . . a murder which the Mayor and police
perpetrated without the shadow of necessity.[1]

The East St. Louis riot of 1917 was no less horrendous. The *Report
of the National Advisory Commission on Civil Disorders* notes the
following:

The next day a Negro was shot on the main street, and a
new riot was underway. The area became a "bloody half
mile" for 3 or 4 hours; streetcars were stopped, and Negroes,
without regard to age or sex, were pulled off and stoned,
clubbed, and kicked, and mob leaders calmly shot and killed
Negroes who were lying in the blood in the street. As the
victims were placed in an ambulance, the crowds cheered
and applauded.[2]

Moreover, "Police did little more than take the injured to hospitals
and disarm Negroes."[3] These are only two of a number of accounts
of police involvement in crimes against the minority person.

Unfortunately, such conduct on the part of the police continued. The 1935 Harlem Riot Commission reported police repression as a contributing factor to that riot. Police action frequently
precipitated riots within black communities following World War
II. In the disorders studied by the Kerner Commission, the "overwhelming majority of the civilians killed and injured were Negroes."[4] The Los Angeles Police Department was responsible for
16 of the 26 deaths ruled justifiable homicide in the Watts Riot
(the National Guard was responsible for another seven).[5] While
90 Los Angeles policemen were hurt in this riot, 773 civilians were
injured.[6]

As a response to reported sniping in Newark, over 20 blacks
(including six women and two children) were killed by police,
one youth being shot 45 times.[7] Of those killed, 10 were slain
"inside or just outside their homes."[8]

The military, especially the Newark Police, not only triggered
the riot . . . but then created a climate of opinion that supported the use of all necessary force to suppress the riot.[9]

Lawyers, constitutional law professors, and American Civil Liberties Union representatives reported that Newark police engaged

in a pattern of systematic violence, terror, abuse, intimidation . . . they seized on the initial disorders as an opportunity and pretext to perpetrate the most horrendous and widespread killing, violence, torture, and intimidation, not in response to any crime or civilian disorder. . . .[10]

The Kerner Commission found that almost invariably the incident that ignites disorder arises from police action."[11]

A critical variable in the nature of minority-police relations seems to be "Who initiates the contact?" Because so many minority persons view the police with distrust, if not hostility, a minority person is less likely to originate the contact than is the policeman. Thus the attitude of the initiating officer is very important. When queried by members of the President's Crime Commission Task Force on Police, 72 percent of the police officers interviewed in three major cities showed prejudice against blacks.[12] One study, for example, found that in precincts primarily comprised of blacks, over three-fourths of the policemen expressed prejudice against blacks, while only 1 percent expressed sympathetic attitudes.[13]

Of all the 76 reported race riots in the 50-year period preceding 1965, the second most common precipitating incident was the arrest of blacks or offense by whites against blacks.[14]

If there is a disturbing similarity between the account of the Newark Riot and General Sheridan's account of the New Orleans mob action approximately 100 years earlier, it serves to emphasize the continuity in the negative nature of police-minority interaction.

While it is wise to exercise discretion in projecting trends from anecdotes, police involvement with minority peoples has so frequently been either excessive or negligent that one concludes unequal protection of minorities is the rule, not the exception. This judgment validates for the member of a minority group his right to view law enforcement with hostility and distrust.

Although the report of the Kerner Commission dealt largely with attitudes and feelings of "ghetto" residents, samplings of blacks in higher income brackets reveal no differences in attitudes and opinions as they relate to unequal protection. The term *unequal* includes all behaviors of the white police officer as these attitudes, feelings, and overt actions and reactions pertain to the black citizen. It is common knowledge that in most situations, when talk is about "black culture," "black values," and the like, no distinction is made between the university graduate and the illiterate black or, sometimes, the common criminal.

Policemen approach minority group members cautiously—
alert for danger. The factor of race is clearly a specific cue
in the policeman's world. Policemen associate minority status
with a high incidence of crime, especially crimes against the
person, with bodily harm to police officers, and with a general
lack of support for the police. But minority people are also
peculiarly visible to policemen because of the way in which
policemen think. Policemen are attuned to incongruity, a judgment which involves fitting people against their immediate
surroundings. Incongruity is the ground for a policeman's
suspicions. Because they are minority people, they are bound
to appear discordant to policemen in most of the environment
of a middle-class, white society. For this reason they doubly
draw the attention of police officers.[15]

Not surprisingly, therefore, a recent research project placing Black
Panther stickers on cars whose drivers never had a ticket over
years of driving had to be abandoned within a week because of
the number of tickets issued and the threats made against these
drivers.

A senior police officer explains:

Pretty soon you decide they're all just niggers and they'll
never be anything else but niggers. It would take not just
an average man to resist this feeling, it would take an extraordinary man to resist it, and there are few ways by which
the police department can attract extraordinary men to join
it.[16]

This attitude is expressed widely by both junior and senior officers
and appears to become an "acceptable and justified" reaction. As
chiefs of police or their command officers accept it and the resulting
behaviors on the part of their men, they must begin defending
unequal treatment, whether in fact they do or do not consider
it professional or ethical.

The only way to police a ghetto is to be oppressive. None
of the Police Commissioner's men, even with the best will
in the world, have any way of understanding the lives led
by the people; they swagger about in twos and threes patrol-
ling. Their very presence is an insult, and it would be, even
if they spent their entire day feeding gumdrops to children.
They represent the force of the white world, and that world's

real intentions are, simply, for that world's criminal profit
and ease, to keep the black man corralled up here, in this
place. The badge, the gun in the holster, and the swinging
club, make vivid what will happen should this rebellion become overt. . . . It is hard, on the other hand, to blame the
policeman, blank, good-natured, thoughtless, and insuperably
innocent, for being such a perfect representative of the people
he serves. He, too, believes in good intentions and is
astounded and offended when they are not taken for the deed.
He has never, himself, done anything for which to be hated—
which of us has? And yet he is facing, daily and nightly,
the people who would gladly see him dead, and he knows
it; there is no way for him not to know it. There are few
things under heaven more unnerving than the silent, accumu-
lating contempt and hatred of a people. He moves through
Harlem, therefore, like an occupying soldier in a bitterly
hostile country; which is precisely what, and where, he is,
and is the reason he walks in twos and threes.[17]

Consequently, police–minority group relations frequently assume an adversary nature, with the policeman and the minority
citizen each losing respect for the other and having the disrespect
mutually reinforced.

Although much is made of the abrasive relationship between
black citizens and police, it is increasingly obvious that other minorities are beginning to express more open hostility toward police.
A national survey on police-community relations found that "Latin
Americans also tend to look upon the police as enemies who protect
only the white power structure."[18] The Committee for Justice, a
group said to be composed of "various minority and chicano organizations" published this "Guest Viewpoint" in a southwestern
newspaper (the *Daily Texan,* November 17, 1973):

In 1970 the U.S. Commission on Civil Rights after nearly
three years of uninvestigation concluded that there existed
". . . evidence of widespread patterns of police misconduct
against Mexican Americans in the Southwest." To be sure,
chicanos hardly needed anyone to tell them that such maltreatment existed. But at long last, clear and irrefutable documentation had been gathered to prove a long-standing allegation. As in the case with most such commissions, many recommendations to remedy this situation were proposed. Evidence
from the last three years, however, indicates that nothing
has been done.

Examining the situation outside the state of Texas clearly demonstrates that police violence against chicanos has continued unabated. Ruben Salazar, Francisco Garcia, Mario Baneras and Juan De La Cruz in California. Bobby Garcia, Tony Lopez, Felipe Mares, Roy Gallegos, Antonio Cordova and Juan Garcia in New Mexico. And the list reads on and on. Over 20 unarmed, defenseless chicanos murdered by police since the commission report in 1970. And still nothing is done.

Law enforcement agencies in Texas have done little better than the rest of their southwestern counterparts. Victor Nava, Mario Benavides, Alfonso Flores, Magdaleno Dimas, Rodolfo Santillan, and most recently and blantly, of course, Santos Rodriguez, have all died at the hands of "Texas' finest." Truly the Texas Rangers are no longer needed—the police now are doing their work for them. What's more, no police officer has ever been convicted for murdering or assaulting a chicano. If the reader thinks chicanos have fared better here in Austin, then read on.

As recently as 1971 we have the cases of Joe Cedillo, Jr. and Ignacio Lara. Both teenagers were killed by police in a highly suspect manner. In the first incident, the youth was shot in the back as he ran from a grocery store carrying a loaf of bread and a package of bologna. Lara died of internal injuries which police said resulted from his falling when they chased him. Both cases resulted in no recrimination of any kind against the police officers.

In almost every case mentioned, as well as many left unmentioned, the chicano community has reacted strongly against such injustice. The agencies of law enforcement, however, have chosen to ignore such complaints. At long last the chicano community is saying, ENOUGH! We will no longer tolerate such inhumane and racist treatment on the part of those designated to "protect" us. With this in mind a massive rally is being planned for 2 P.M. Saturday at the State Capitol as the beginning of an organized and continuing effort to cease police maltreatment of chicanos, blacks and other minorities. Such speakers as Jose Angel Gutierrez, Ramsey Muniz, Marta Cotera, Velma Roberts and others have agreed to take part. Immediately following the rally, a meeting is scheduled for speakers and interested individuals to coordinate a conference concerning minorities and law enforcement to be held in the near future. This conference will attempt to deal with various aspects of administration of justice in realistic and concrete fashion. It is evident that simple words will not suffice. Similarly, action without prepared strategy is meaning-less. Planned, well thought-out and coordinated action is our proposal for terminating police misconduct toward minorities. We sincerely hope everyone will attend the rally and the meetings afterward.[19]

Police officers express both surprise and shock at the growing number of confrontations between themselves and Mexican-American youth. In human relations training group sessions policemen have made such statements as these: "I never expected those Mexicans to act that way. They are usually very quiet and very docile. We don't ever have any trouble with them. I don't understand what's happening to them." One officer said, "They're acting just like the blacks. It all goes to show what effect violence among blacks is having upon people that usually don't buck the law."

Other men on the force expressed surprise because they could see no reason for this hostility among the Mexican-American population. As far as the officers were concerned, Mexican-Americans were seen as white and treated "just like white folks." However, reports of the Civil Rights Commission offer proof that conditions, particularly in the Southwest, are not good for the Mexican-American. His lot is complicated by a language barrier and often a distinct cultural difference. These facts are viewed seriously by the Mexican-American community, since they may have a subtle effect upon the treatment received from some law enforcement bodies. Certainly, the situation is at least blurred by what seems to be a difference in attitude between some members of the older and younger generations.

One officer let an attitude slip when he said, "Well, it won't take long to put them back in their place. It's just a bunch of those young hot-heads. The older folks know better." Many individuals feel that there is no concern about understanding the reason for the new aggressiveness. All attention seemed to be focused upon immediately quelling disturbances and keeping the lid on.

It is obvious also that the Mexican-American has suffered from a stereotype that pictures him as docile, peace-loving, law-abiding, nonthreatening, and lackadaisical. Unfortunately this stereotype is and has been reinforced in many ways. Only recently has the Mexican-American, like the black, sought to have removed from advertisements, motion pictures, and the like objectionable material that portrays him in demeaning roles. Negative perceptions of individuals is more easily removed from visual material than from the minds of a credulous public. When one person finds his perception of another to be ego-syntonic, he is not likely to readily change his attitude or his behavior based upon that perception, even though he knows it to be erroneous.

It is much easier to deal with a stereotype than to deal with individual differences. Whereas the generalizations permitted by stereotypic thinking allow for a rather accurate prediction of behavior and relatively uniform means of handling that behavior, the acknowledgment of wide differences within and among groups permits neither. It demands depth in both education and training in the area of human behavior and requires a variety of responses appropriate to the different behaviors. For the law enforcement officer it is much easier to deal with the Mexican-American and the black as stereotypes (for his response requires little thought) than to deal with them in the more accurate, but complex, manner necessary when the within-group differences that actually exist are recognized. This, of course, is a problem of training and education of the police officer.

It is a generally accepted fact that the American Indian, or Native American, has received unequal treatment under the law. Whereas this allegation is not questioned as it relates to the American Indian, it is sometimes questioned in relation to the black or Mexican-American. History has largely ignored the treatment accorded blacks and Mexican-Americans but has grudgingly admitted that treaties made with the Indian Nations have not been honored and are still not honored. The legal status of the Native American in his own country can be seen at least as frustrating.

There has been some speculation about the overall situation at Wounded Knee and the status of the Native American in America. The deception historically visited upon the American Indian was obvious at Wounded Knee, but the reaction of law enforcement was interesting. In the recent past, unarmed students (and particularly black students) have been attacked with a vengeance and with the weaponry of war. Many were killed. It was a relief when it became rather obvious that there would be no all-out attack on the small band of armed defenders at Wounded Knee. Whether the Native American poses no real menace to America in the minds of most Americans, or the goals of the Native American seem less threatening than those of the black or Mexican-American, or the Native American has more sympathy and support from Middle America, or law enforcement simply responded in a more enlightened manner, this restraint deserves examination. It is hoped that the latter is responsible for the minimum amount of violence displayed in a situation that could have resulted in much more bloodshed.

What must not be viewed lightly here is the behavior of the Indian. He, too, seemed to feel that attention is drawn to minority group problems only when acts of violence highlight the injustices. The truth that keeps alive the embers of hate is that little has changed for the minority groups as relates to their position in America. Although it appears to be the responsibility of law enforcement to maintain these groups in subjugated and discriminatory positions (at least in the eyes of minority groups), one may logically assume that there will always be some kind of distance between most members of minority groups and law enforcement personnel. Moreover, in light of the facts of recent history, these groups will not expect fair treatment. They will continue to regard instances in which justice has prevailed for minority group persons as rare exceptions rather than the rule for all Americans.

Activist white Americans have come to view law enforcement in much the same manner that it is viewed by minority groups. They have tasted death at the hands of police officers who felt they were carrying out a mandate of society as they fired into groups of activists. They have seen this behavior on the part of police officers as representing the will of middle America. But the activists are resentful that law enforcement agents go to such extremes in carrying out their enforcement duties. The "Kent State" in America will not soon be forgotten. Only studied, viable acts highlighting the fact that the quality of mercy in America is not strained will gradually ease the erosion of faith in our system of justice and remove fear of the law enforcement officer.

Even Mr. Average American has some fear of the person who enforces the law and wants to stay "on his good side." It may be only that the citizen does not want his good record of public morals or law-abiding character blemished, but seeing a policeman is enough to put him on the alert. His apprehension and insecurity are heightened in these days of patrol cars.

A number of cities are returning to foot patrols. There seems to be a feeling that on foot patrol the officer is closer to his public and is a more effective enforcement agent in some situations. To many citizens, it is a trend toward the "good old days" when people often aspired to be policemen. Their major role was seen as that of fighting crime, especially organized crime. In the South, unfortunately, there was still the fun of "keeping the nigger in his place," and in the small towns and hamlets it was a matter of unquestioned authority and white supremacy. As late as the 1930s, in a Chicago interview one baseball player on the New York Yankees' team was asked what he did during the off-season. He stated that he was a policeman down South. When asked about the job, he explained

with great humor how he enjoyed "beating niggers on the head."
Of course, this national broadcast gained him no friends among
the black population, but also there were few angry cries of resentment toward his attitude from his colleagues or many other whites.
There is no public record of his being suspended or otherwise
sharply reprimanded.

Nonetheless, except for the molesting of young black girls
by unscrupulous officers, even the Negro had not too much to
fear as long as he "stayed in his place" and did not "raise any
fuss" when preyed upon physically by whites.

It is almost unimaginable, but some of this same situation
reported prevails even today in certain sections of the rural South.
Parts of the Midwest (particularly sourthern Illinois and southern
Indiana) are said to be copies of the rural South in this respect,
but there appears not to be the blatant evidence of such police
misconduct, except as reported in East St. Louis and its environs.
Stories of outright murders of blacks and Mexican-Americans leak
out of small towns from time to time, but there is no way to
get proof positive or even to uncover enough evidence for a valid
investigation because of the alleged fear on the part of the minority
residents. Even if such evidence is gathered, only in recent years
has any type of punishment been meted out to the guilty. Minorities
feel that, in the case of police officers, who will find them guilty?
With the long-established and validated history of brutal behavior
among the so-called protectors of society, what chance does the
professional, honest, and fair sheriff or city policeman have to
change the bad image? Too often society seems to condone it.
Thus, again the minority group or poor person feels vulnerable
and unprotected.

Our system of law and justice must be a viable means for
equal protection by the law regardless of race, economic stat.s,
or any other such variable. Our country must be safe for its citizens
and must foster the democratic principles (protected by the police
officers) of life, liberty, and the pursuit of happiness, or distrust
and hate will continue to grow.

Even the chief of police finds it difficult to rectify the abuses
of the officer on the beat. He apologizes, "It is hard to wipe out
prejudice. We know we have prejudiced men, but they are good
officers otherwise and we hope they'll change." With what is seen
as little incentive to change and only wrist-slapping in even the
most blatant cases of misconduct, why should policemen seek to
be "extraordinary"? An easier way of dealing with minority people
is to ignore them as much as possible. Of course, this means inadequate protection for minority neighborhoods.

Numerous studies have indicated the need for more protection in minority areas. In Watts, where 41 percent of the blacks surveyed indicated that police were not doing a good job or that they were doing a poor job, lack of adequate protection was the basis for their opinions rather than discrimination or brutality.[20] Permissive law enforcement and lack of provision for adequate protection in areas occupied by blacks rate as the main criticisms of police by minority groups in this country. According to the U.S. Civil Rights Commission, in Cleveland "the most frequent complaint [of Negroes] is that of permissive law enforcement and that policemen fail to provide adequate protection and service in areas occupied by Negroes."[21]

Likewise, commission staff were told that Mexican-Americans, especially the migrant workers, in rural areas found it difficult to obtain police protection when needed.

Our legal system is viewed as compensating for underprotecting minorities by overprosecuting them. For instance, while over one-half of the convicted rapists in the South are white, 87 percent of those executed for rape between 1930 and 1963 were black.[22] Correspondingly, minority people are prosecuted more vigorously for crimes against whites than are whites for crimes against them. Insufficient protection of minorities is further indicated by the fact that black women are 18 times more likely than white women to be raped.[23]

Not surprisingly, therefore, the Commission on Civil Disorders states:

> For nonwhites, the probability of suffering from any index of crime except larceny is 78% higher than for whites. The probability of being raped is 3.7% higher among nonwhite women, and the probability of being robbed is 3.5% higher for nonwhites in general.[24]

Thus, crime flourishes in minority areas. The Task Force on Human Rights found overwhelming evidence that "Negroes are disproportionately the victims of crimes."[25] Interviews with minority persons representing a wide cross section of the work world and the various socioeconomic levels reveal that underenforcement of the law is resented by minority groups as much as is overenforcement. Toleration by the police of illegal drug activities, prostitution, and street violence enrages minority residents. Studies have indicated the dual standard of law enforcement for whites and minority persons, a duality inherent in the societal context surrounding the police officer.

Ignorance on the part of the general public along with distorted statistical reports serve to exacerbate an already unhealthy situation. As an example, these remarks were made on television by a white member of a certain Texas community: "Blacks make up about 23% of our population, but *they* commit 80% of our crimes. Why shouldn't we be suspicious of *all* blacks?" As stated, this is the case; but no one explains that figures show roughly *1 percent* of the black population to be involved in that *80 percent* of the crimes. Recidivism caused by laxity in protection of the community accounts for the figures, but no one takes time to point out to a fearful citizenry. No mention is made of the large numbers of law-abiding blacks who are forced by discriminatory laws and acts to live largely in constricted areas ravaged by crime. They suffer most because these crimes by blacks are crimes *against* blacks. Seldom is this fact revealed. When it is brought out, the naive simply say, "Why don't they move?" or "Why don't they do something about it?" Move where? Do what?

The federal government has refused to issue more than a weak *moral* statement about housing that would permit blacks to overcome even subtle acts of discrimination and to live wherever they desire and can afford. Yes, crime is greater in black neighborhoods; but blacks are the victims, and a very small percentage of blacks continue to prey upon other blacks. Crime by blacks against blacks remains a joke to many officers. Only when that crime is committed against a white (unless he is a hippie or a leftist) do minority groups feel that the keepers of the peace swing into real action.

This attitude certainly is not displayed by *all* police officers, but it is so overwhelming and those in opposition to the neglecting and unethical behavior are seemingly so impotent that the average black feels *no* policeman really cares. Hence the lack of cooperation with police among blacks. There is no real, honest show of concern for crime in black communities except as it directly affects some white interest.

> No policeman enforces all the laws of a community. If he
> did, we would all be in jail before the end of the first day.
> The laws which are selected for enforcement are those which
> the power structure of the community wants enforced. The
> police official's job is dependent upon his having radar-like
> equipment to sense what is the power structure and what
> it wants enforced as a law.[26]

In our society, where the structure to which the policeman is accountable is white, his unequal protection of minorities is said to be accepted and even expected. While police often project indifference to problems occurring in minority neighborhoods, the same problems are quickly addressed if occurring in white areas. For example, police will respond to disorderly conduct in a white bar but when called to a disturbance in a black bar will say, "I don't believe in serving as a bar owner's bouncer." Likewise, police have been known to say, "Let them kill each other off," when referring to murders among minorities. For minority persons, the choice is all too often underenforcement or overenforcement. Thus, if a policeman even notices a Mexican-American staggering, "it is because of narcotics, but when an Anglo staggers, they call a doctor. . . ."[27]

This double standard of law enforcement is obvious to minority people working in white neighborhoods and constantly seeing those areas protected. The minority person living in a white neighborhood and aware of the protection available to him is even more aware of the lack of protection when he goes into a black or brown neighborhood. For reasons of income or *de facto* segregation, many minority people find themselves forced to reside in neighborhoods where equal and efficient enforcement occurs on their television screens weekly, but not on their streets daily.

Police officers are members of society and are citizens like everyone else. It is no wonder, then, that they labor under the erroneous conclusion that blacks may live anywhere they want since laws have been passed protecting that right. Large numbers of Americans cling to this old idea despite accounts in newspapers and on radio and television regarding prominent blacks who are not permitted to live in certain neighborhoods or who are harassed to the extent that they must move. It is preferable to look at those who are living in predominately white neighborhoods and to point with a kind of questionable pride at this "accomplishment." Many blacks live in predominately white neighborhoods and indicate that they are very happy in their living situation. In fact, many have talked about how wonderful their white neighbors are and the fact that these neighbors have quickly learned how to treat them just as they would any other neighbor. That is to say, they are not overly solicitous, nor are they hostile because of their recognizing that the individual happens to be black. Rather, they extend the hand of friendship and behave in a normal manner.

However, in some of these situations it is not clear how long the blacks were uneasy, or how much time elapsed before they were able to sleep comfortably without expecting a brick to be tossed through the window or receiving a threatening telephone call. It would be interesting to know the number of blacks who live in mainly white neighborhoods but who spent many a restless night before they were certain that they were accepted as neighbors and as Americans by those living around them. Unquestionably, these blacks would have been much more comfortable had they been assured of protection by the police in the case of harassment or damage to their property or to themselves. They could not be *assured* of a proper response should they complain about discriminatory practices of their neighbors.

In a city in the Southwest, for example, this incident is reported: The child of a black family who recently moved into a white neighborhood was beaten with chains by white students and threatened with bodily harm by white parents. In addition, the black parents found a black cat with its throat cut in their mailbox one morning and they received threatening telephone calls. The response of one police officer who reported to their call for help was "How long have you lived here?" Told that this family had lived in this city for a number of years, he commented that they should know this kind of thing happens and would happen under these conditions and he could see no reason for their complaining. Only after several appeals and intervention by the news media was something concrete done about the situation. Similar incidents have been repeated in cities across the country. Some blacks moving into white neighborhoods arm themselves prior to moving their families into the new home. When asked about this the reply has been, "We don't expect any help from the police so we are going to have to protect ourselves."

One look at the living patterns in our cities discloses that segregated housing still obtains. Even the most uninformed person knows that with the status and upward mobility situation in the United States most people want to improve their living conditions. They have failed to do so, in many instances, not because they did not have the money, but because they did not want to find themselves in a dangerous situation and unprotected by the law enforcement agency in their community. When people live together, they learn to make assessments not on the basis of color but on the basis of behavior. When this opportunity is not permitted on account of violence on the part of whites and little or no protection by the law enforcement establishment, the possibility of our finally becoming one society with equal justice for all becomes remote.

Some law enforcement officials have asked why blacks do not file more complaints against individuals who intimidate or persecute them. To most blacks and members of other minority groups it seems ridiculous to file a complaint when there is a serious question as to whether the law under which you file your complaint will be enforced. The history of selective enforcement in this country—a selective enforcement that has been validated—gives most blacks no reason to believe that in their particular case they will receive a fair hearing, if any hearing at all.

Senator Robert F. Kennedy said, "Laws confer 'rights' only on those who can articulate a claim before some authority who will enforce it."[28] For many minority persons, unequal enforcement of the law negates their rights under those laws. Again, it is true that minority group individuals have complained before authority, have been heard, and have won their cases. But unfortunately this tends to be an exception rather than the rule. When the articulation of a claim by minority group persons receives the same attention that the articulation of a claim by a middle-class white individual receives, we will be moving toward a type of society envisioned by Martin Luther King, Jr. Perfection in this situation probably will not be achieved because of the number of variables that obtain, but all individuals will have faith that a strong effort is being made by those who formulate, interpret, and carry out the law.

> Every man brings human rights into society with him—society
> does not bestow them. But society does sometimes violate
> them, or takes measures that threaten their free exercise by
> all citizens, or, more invidiously, by some citizens. Today
> in America some human rights are threatened for all, and
> some are violated for some.[29]

There is and has been sufficient evidence of unequal protection for minority groups over the years. The trend is changing, but much too slowly. Moral leadership in the top echelon of law enforcement agencies seems to be lacking. Either these persons don't care or it is personally expedient for them not to rock the boat. They don't want criticism from either City Hall or the men serving under their command. The rule seems to be "Give them [blacks] enough protection to keep them quiet; then go on with the more important job of protecting white interests." Little or nothing is said about officials who are trying to bring equal protection of the law to their communities. There are some indications that they are harassed or even intimidated to the point of resigning or remaining silent.

Recent national moves by blacks actively to support police are an encouraging sign. Not only are organizations moving about the country urging active support of law enforcement, but black votes are outnumbering other votes on issues dealing with pay, pensions, and the like for police and firemen.

Heretofore, efforts by blacks to cooperate with white law enforcement in some areas have been ignored, or unmitigated bigotry has prevailed. This may be the last chance for police officers to join hands with a group for both their own betterment and that of the concerned minority population. The kind of support here is diametrically opposed to the kind of support offered by certain other groups that seek to use the policeman. Theirs is a philosophy of infiltration and ultimate takeover to "save the country from communism." The philosophy of the black is not infiltration and takeover to save the country from communism. Rather, it is an endeavor to help save the country from itself.

To deny equal protection for *all* is to violate the basic rights guaranteed by the Constitution of the United States. Such denial transcends the obvious restrictions on *civil rights* and, in a dangerous and insidious manner, erodes the *human rights* of all Americans. Pointing fearful fingers at the dangers of communism while taking a giant step toward fascism is no safeguard for democracy. The American ideal can accommodate neither communism nor fascism.

The democratic process as expounded by Thomas Jefferson and as described in countless documents is accepted by most Americans as the ultimate means of achieving individual freedoms and the high goal of the right to life, liberty, and the pursuit of happiness, regardless of race, ethnicity, religion, or other differentiating variables. None of this is possible if the germane values so well *described* by document are not vigorously *defined* by law. If the minority does not possess equal rights protected by equal law, oppression does indeed prevail.

EXCESSIVE DISCRIMINATORY USE OF FORCE

"Police brutality!" was almost a rallying cry in the past. There was so much evidence of violence against the person by some police officers that no one denied this fact—including officers themselves. Rather it was said that they changed the terminology to the less-harsh-sounding "excessive, discriminatory use of force." Then, many tried to explain that away. This charge, because of its nature, was more destructive to the law enforcement image than any other.

There is documented material presenting numerous cases of police brutality. Not only has television vividly portrayed excessive use of force by police officers but investigating bodies (both private and federally appointed) have produced unimpeachable, though disheartening, evidence of it.

Despite the reports, many officials either ignored, disavowed, or explained away this anathema to proper law enforcement procedure. One chief of police said that, at the most, police brutality is only a lack of good judgment on the part of the offending officer. Uninformed and lethargic America dismisses it by saying, "They probably deserved it!" Grand juries have a questionable record of dismissals or "no-bills" in such cases. Federal grand juries have a little better record, but only in the face of overwhelming evidence. When there were convictions, the punishment, in the eyes of numerous Americans, was seen as quite inadequate. The feeling is that most law enforcement personnel appear to know that they are above the law in most serious cases.

If this indictment is not true, the meager evidence to the contrary must be explained. It behooves law enforcement to regain the confidence particularly of its minority (and, more than realized, majority) public. There is no reason that, like other professional organizations, it should not have a publicly spelled-out code of ethics and a regulatory body to ensure strict adherence at all levels. This would seem more necessary for the field of law enforcement than for any other profession. It would eliminate some of the need for the global defensive stature of police officers that weakens the confidence of earnestly concerned citizens.

> The typical Southern policeman is thus a low-paid and dependent man, with little general education or special police schooling. His social prestige is low. But he is the local representative of the law; he has authority and may at any time resort to the use of his gun. It is not difficult to understand that this economically and socially insecure man, given this tremendous and dangerous authority, continually feels himself on the defensive.[30]

Further documentation may be appropriate at this time. Rose says of the policeman in the Negro neighborhood:

> This weak man with his strong weapons—backed by all of the authority of white society—is now sent to be the white law in the Negro neighborhood. His social heritage has taught him to despise Negroes, and he has had little education which could have changed him. His professional experiences with criminals, prostitutes, and loiterers in Negro joints are strongly selective and only magnify his prejudices. The result is that probably no group of whites in America has a lower opinion

of the Negro people and is more fixed in its views than
Southern policemen.

In many, but not all, Southern communities, Negroes complain indignantly about police brutality. . . . The most publicized type of police brutality is the extreme case of Negroes
being killed by policemen. This phenomenon is important
in itself, but it constitutes only a minor portion of all police
brutality, and the information available on Negro killings by
the police does not give a reliable index of the wider phenomenon. A perhaps un-typical example for the Border states,
but not unusual for many areas in the Deep South, comes
from Baltimore between 1938 and 1942, when nine Negroes
were killed by police officers. The majority of police killings
of Negroes must be deemed unnecessary when measured by
a decent standard of policemanship.[31]

Many police departments permit observers to ride on patrol.
The following incident is reported by one:

On a Friday in the middle of July, the observer arrived for
the 4 to 12 midnight watch. The beat car that had been
randomly chosen carried two white patrolmen—one with 14
years of experience in the precinct, the other with three.

The watch began rather routinely as the policemen cruised
the district. Their first radio dispatch came at about 5:30
P.M. They were told to investigate two drunks in a cemetery.
On arriving they found two white men "sleeping one off."
Without questioning the men, the older policeman began to
search one of them, ripping his shirt and hitting him in the
groin with a nightstick. The younger policeman, as he
searched the second, ripped away the seat of his trousers,
exposed his buttocks. The policeman then prodded the men
toward the cemetery fence and forced them to climb it, laughing at the plight of the drunk with the exposed buttocks.
As the drunks went over the fence, one policeman shouted,
"I ought to run you fuckers in!" The other remarked to the
observer, "Those assholes won't be back; a bunch of shitty
winos."

Not long after they returned to their car, the policemen
stopped a woman who had made a left turn improperly. She
was treated very politely, and the younger policeman, who
wrote the ticket, later commented to the observer, "Nice lady."
At 7:30 they were dispatched to check a suspicious auto.
After a quick check, the car was marked abandoned.

Shortly after a 30-minute break for a 7:30 "lunch," the two policemen received a dispatch to take a burglary report. Arriving at a slum walkup, the police entered a room where an obviously drunk white man in his late 40's insisted that someone had entered and stolen his food and liquor. He kept insisting that it had been taken and that he had been forced to borrow money to buy beer. The younger policeman, who took the report, kept harassing the man, alternating between mocking and badgering him with rhetorical questions. "You say your name is Half-A-Wit (for Hathaway)? Do you sleep with niggers? How did you vote on the bond issue? Are you sure that's all that's missing? Are you a virgin yet?" The man responded to all of this with the seeming vagueness and joviality of the intoxicated, expressing gratitude for the policemen's help as they left. The older policeman remarked to the observer as they left, "Ain't drunks funny?"

For the next hour little happened, but as the two were moving across the precinct shortly after 10 P.M., a white man and a woman in their 50's flagged them down. Since they were obviously "substantial" middle-class citizens of the district, the policemen listened to their complaints that a Negro man was causing trouble inside the public-transport station from which they had just emerged. The woman said that he had sworn at her. The older policeman remarked, "What's a nigger doing up here? He should be down on Franklin Road."

With that, they ran into the station and grabbed the Negro man who was inside. Without questioning him, they shoved him into a phone booth and began beating him with their fists and a flashlight. They also hit him in the groin. They dragged him out and kept him on his knees. He pleaded that he had just been released from a mental hospital that day and, begging not to be hit again, asked them to let him return to the hospital. One policeman said: "Don't you like us, nigger? I like to beat niggers and rip out their eyes." They took him outside to their patrol car. Then they decided to put him on a bus, telling him that he was returning to the hospital; they deliberately put him on a bus going in the opposite direction. Just before the Negro boarded the bus, he said, "You police just like to shoot and beat people." The first policeman replied, "Get moving, nigger, or I'll shoot you." The man was crying and bleeding as he was put on the bus. Leaving the scene, the younger policeman commented, "He won't be back."

For the rest of the evening, the two policemen kept looking
for drunks and harassing any they found. They concluded
the evening by being dispatched to an address where, they
were told, a man was being held for the police. No one an-
swered their knock. They left.[32]

Although there were encouraging stories of officers' lending
assistance to citizens, many observers either stated that they felt
this to be an exception or talked about the degree to which the
harassment or brutality overshadowed the professional behaviors
and seemed to be supported by administrators.

The reader, as well as most police administrators, may be
skeptical about reports that policemen used force in the presence of observers. Indeed, one police administrator, indignant
over reports of undue use of force in his department, seemed
more concerned that the policemen had permitted themselves
to be observed behaving improperly than he was about their
improper behavior. When demanding to know the names of
policemen who had used force improperly so he could discharge them—a demand we could not meet, since we were
bound to protect our sources of information—he remarked,
"Any officer who is stupid enough to behave that way in
the presence of outsiders deserves to be fired."[33]

The situation for the Mexican-American has been equally dis-
mal, especially in small towns, as was stated earlier. Cases were
cited in the hearing before the U.S. Commission on Civil Rights,
San Antonio, Texas, December 9–14, 1968, that involved beatings
of Mexican-Americans by law enforcement officials, including some
judges. One need only read *Mexican-Americans and the Administration of Justice in the Southwest* (U.S. Commission on Civil
Rights, March 1970) for documentation of the state of the judiciary
system as it relates to the rights of the Mexican-American.

Not until recently has any real effort been made to teach
Spanish to officers who work in areas where they have more than
average contact with Spanish-speaking persons. The language barrier must arouse extreme anxiety in the individual who finds himself
confronted by a policeman (and more especially a small-town
sheriff) to whom he cannot make himself understood. Not only
does he become a victim of ridicule and personal debasement but
he may be immobilized by his fears, exposing himself to the charge
of resisting arrest or using abusive language.

In the case of the Mexican-American (as with the black)
brutality will continue as long as nothing is done to stop it. Records

of well-documented instances of raw, unmitigated brutality show case after case "dismissed" or "still under investigation" until "time takes care of it." One case brought before the commission included firsthand testimony from a nurse who saw a highway patrolman strike one of two Mexican-American women. The nurse reported that she heard the officer say, "Come on, come on, who wants to be next?" The officer denied the charge. When asked how the victim received her wound, the officer stated that he had no idea. The incident happened on June 9, 1968. As of March 31, 1969, it was still under investigation despite eyewitness accounts by a professional person.

In another case involving the beating of a Mexican-American by a sheriff and a judge, the case was dismissed by the Department of Justice because (in the opinion of the department) it lacked prosecutive merit since the victim's statements were uncorroborated.

Officers have admitted that many keep "throw-downs" so that if they kill an unarmed person they can present so-called evidence that they were attacked. This sort of thing makes it difficult for the officer who *really* is attacked and who kills in self-defense! His second thought about his partner's murderous act in a time of crisis for himself could cost him his life. There is some feeling among police that officers should not be permitted to carry non-authorized weapons while on duty.

Illustrative are the results of a study of physical force exercised by the police against citizens in three major cities. Improper force was used 37 times in a seven-week period.[34] Forty-four citizens were assaulted by the police, and in 15 of these cases no arrests were made; in 8 of them *no* verbal or physical resistance was offered.[35]

While arrests were made in 22 of the 37 incidents, force was applied in two cases when no verbal or physical resistance was made, and in five situations the policeman used force *after* subduing a resisting offender.[36] Although the citizen appeared only physically bruised in about one-half of the cases, citizens were hospitalized in three instances.[37]

One-third of the observed cases of excessive force occurred within the police station, including two of the three cases requiring hospitalization.[38] Significantly, while 18 percent of situations involving suspects finally terminated at the station, 32 percent of the situations involving excessive force occurred in the station.[39]

Most disturbing is the fact that even the FBI seldom helps the "little man" subjected to excessive, discriminatory use of force because "we need the cooperation of and must work closely with local law enforcement people." U.S. civil rights commissions and civil rights divisions of various agencies get bogged down in legal entanglements and seldom prove effective in doing more than investigating and from time to time exposing. Many cases are never even filed because the victim fears reprisal—and justifiably so. Where the victim has won, often he still loses because of the harassment that follows his victory.

The kind of material presented in this section of the chapter can be duplicated many times and in many other publications. It is highly sensitive and is an indictment not so much against those who perpetrate the crime of police brutality as against a system and a public that permit it. The victims usually are too poor and/or too frightened to get relief or they have given up any hope that there is justice (except in rare and extreme cases) in our system of government. This attitude is to be lamented, because it implies a breakdown in law and justice, not at the citizen level but at the very top. Where a judiciary system spawns the criminal and dismisses the criminal act if it is committed by one of its own (again except in a few cases), the image of democracy and justice is severely tarnished.

The situation is changing, but too slowly. This is an area of human concern that cannot easily tolerate slow change because of its fundamental place in human society.

DISCOURTESY

Discourtesy from police is expected by most blacks and other minority groups, as well as by poor whites. Only a few persons from the total population report such behavior. Almost no blacks openly complain. While the power of the police officer may be restricted on paper, in actuality (particularly on the streets), it is virtually absolute. He is permitted to employ "whatever force is necessary to subdue." Many teenaged blacks and Mexican-Americans have been killed and the implicated officer was exonerated because he "thought the youth had a weapon." However, apologies could hardly bring back the lives of the innocent. Knowing that officers have the power to kill and that some will not hesitate to use it, most blacks feel lucky to get off with just verbal abuse.

Some persons explain away discourtesy by blaming it on bad days or seeing it as characteristic of typical police officers. There may be a plausible excuse for discourteous behavior but there is never an acceptable reason. It is a fact that lawbreakers often incite officers to unprofessional conduct by their own behavior, but the policeman must remember that everyone resents being wrong and getting caught. Bearing the brunt of the citizen's rage is always a hazard of the job. Remembering a trite statement and employing its wisdom should be his response: "A soft tongue turneth away wrath." No one excuses unseeming behavior on the part of citizens who are stopped for violations of the law, but even this does not excuse discourtesy. How can one who gives no respect expect respect? Courtesy, like respect, is a two-way street.

There are numerous reports from citizens, irate at being stopped for a traffic violation, who addressed the police officer with verbal abuse but were greeted in return by firm but courteous words. These individuals have admitted their embarrassment and very often apologized to the officer. Although it is difficult to handle extremely abusive language and verbal threats, the professional officer realizes that he has sufficient recourse through law should his own powers of persuasion fail. There is never an excuse for discourtesy.

The use of pejoratives, emotion-laden words, racial slurs, harsh language, curt remarks, and the like, serves only to blemish further an already damaged police image. To many individuals verbal abuse is more anger-producing than any other type of aggressive behavior by police. It can be dehumanizing, leaving the victim with feelings of helpfulness, frustration, or impotent rage. The increase in murders of police officers should be a strong indication not always of simple disrespect for law but of retaliation against anyone in blue for what undesirable officers have done. Strong penalties for killing a police officer will not stop this kind of crime as long as it is encouraged by some and condoned by others. Very often the law-abiding citizen is aroused by the wanton slaying of an officer, but one may hear him say, "Some of those police officers ask for it. It is too bad that they don't get the ones who deserve it and let the good ones live." Good, professional officers pay with their lives for the misconduct of other officers— and many do so simply because of careless, unwarranted discourtesy through harassment, verbal abuse, or disrespect on the part of the unprofessional law enforcement person. Whatever consolation the officer may get as a result of his emotional unloading on a citizen, the outcome is not worth it for him or for the profession.

HARASSMENT

Another form of abuse, more subtle than outright brutality, is police harassment. Harassment is accepted by most law enforcement officers and by many citizens as a necessary method for dealing with some types of criminals. Properly used, this can hardly be denied. However, when this technique is employed by police to satisfy sadistic needs, as a means of getting revenge, or for racial reasons, it can hardly be approved as a rightful or lawful act. It becomes an infringement upon constitutional rights when an officer stops and hassles an interracial couple for no other reason than his personal bigotry. It is no less a violation of human rights when cars bearing groups of young blacks or hippies are constantly stopped, unless the officer really has cause to be suspicious. There are almost no complaints of this nature currently, but the memory of them leaves the individual cautious and somewhat apprehensive.

Intimidation is a more accurate name for illegally stopping, searching, or otherwise harassing innocent persons. Unfortunately, like similar illegal behavior it is difficult to prove intimidation. Knowing this, the unprofessional officer becomes bolder, and innocent victims join the ranks of those who see all police officers as "pigs." As for the criminal, those who are constantly harassed only become more hardened, and those who might be trying to change cease to find reason to continue their efforts to go straight.

In the past few years, harassment has taken on political dimensions. Although not as commonly in the early 1970s as in the middle and late 1960s, one still hears that hippies, "alkies," militant blacks and Mexican-Americans, left-wing students, and others are the victims of some harassment. This kind of intimidating behavior by police officers is usually confined to stopping, seizing, searching, and the like. Police intimidation of homosexual persons because of their life-style, which may be offensive to many but does not violate specific statutes, also has assumed political dimensions in some areas. Because homosexuals represent easy prey for physical assaults and other criminal acts, communities frequented by them are often high-crime areas. Since the homosexual is the object of the crime, if the object is removed, so is the crime. Thus the police can, through either underenforcement or intimidation, deprive citizens of equal protection under the law for indirect cause.

Today, mass arrests have been added to the list of harassment behaviors. In a country that boasts of free speech and freedom of the press, recent actions against even the mildest dissident of just an outspoken newsperson gives one pause. Is harassment becoming (in addition to a tool of law enforcement) a subtle game of political chess? This question haunts many groups—and not just minorities.

Harassment of the police officer by individuals or groups is no more acceptable than police harassment of the citizen. It serves only to generate retaliation that can lead to open conflict. However, unacceptable behavior on the part of individual citizens does not legitimize similar tactics by police. In fact, the law enforcement officer should be trained to handle this kind of offensive, aggressive behavior as one of the hazards of his job. The level of his emotional stability should permit his resentment or anger but afford desirable controls over his reaction. Harassment as a technique should never become harassment or intimidation as a release for sadistic tendencies, bigotry, or revenge. In fact, the police officer has a sufficient number of legal tools at his disposal so that improper, retaliative conduct is never necessary. Again, it must be stressed that police are human and have a right to resent harassment by civilians, but thoughtless reaction can create a bad situation that even time cannot erase.

TREATMENT IN JAILS AND PRISONS

What happens to an individual physically, emotionally, and/or psychologically while incarcerated depends upon many factors. Unless we have an Attica or similar types of serious prison disorders, the general public seems to forget the men and women "behind the walls" or those locked in prison cells across the country. It is as if placing guarded barriers between them and "decent" society suddenly solved problems related to felonies.

However, a closer look at the culture of the convicted, whether through the eyes of history, the writings of inmates and prison officials, or the revealing results of prison and jail riots, might shock the average American and arouse both indignation and some warranted concern within him.

Overall conditions of confinement in all correctional institutions have a disproportionate impact upon blacks—if for no other reason than that of the discriminatory practices which account for their comprising 42 percent of prison rolls (while other nonwhites represent another 22 percent).[40] The recidivism rate is 70 percent.[41]

A point often overlooked when one deals with census figures is racial classification. For example, in speaking of the nonwhites making up that other 22 percent of the prison population one generally means Chinese, Japanese, Indians, and other nonwhites *excluding* Mexican-Americans. The latter have been placed in a kind of schizophrenic census situation. They are at times considered "white" and at other times counted as Mexican-American. This anomalous status serves to exacerbate an identity crisis for some and angers others, but the end result is confusion. If on prison rolls the Mexican-American is classified as "white," the *actual* nonwhite prison population in reality is increased by that number and percentage—making the nonwhite prison population more than 64 percent of the total population of the prison.

Another interesting speculation is that a 70 percent rate of recidivism implies a large number of nonwhite returnees. To these individuals release and imprisonment can seem to be a revolving door designed to reduce white Americans' burden of competing with larger numbers of nonwhites for jobs, housing, education, and other goods and services valued in American society. It may appear to be another vehicle of racism in America.

All of this makes one question both the term *correctional institutions* and the notion that these institutions are designed largely to *rehabilitate* the criminal. The effects of incarceration and the conditions that prevail in the jails and prisons transcend race, religion, ethnicity, and the like. Prisons can dehumanize, harden, and/or destroy the will of an individual or they can act as rehabilitative agents. Naturally, what the institutions become depends upon both the physical environment and the personnel charged with serving them. Environmental inadequacies and improper program planning create an atmosphere conducive to explosion.

There is a growing body of literature that seeks to examine and discuss all aspects of the penal code and penal system. It is not the purpose of this brief section to attempt the absurd task of reviewing or covering completely and in detail all of the findings so carefully documented by others. Our aim is to remind the reader of a few highlights in an effort to indicate the need for public support in endeavors to improve the penal system.

A prisoner's life is ordinarily a numbing round of confinement, supervision, and monotonous underpaid labor. Depending upon his sentence, the days spent away from the outside world can make him fearful of entering that world again, once he is released. In some cases prisoners either break the law in order to be returned to prison life or ask wardens to let them spend the remainder of their lives in the prison culture in one or another capacity.

Others become damaged by overt brutality or subtle, psychological sadistic acts and can hardly wait to be released so they can get revenge on a society that sent them up. Some men and women (for reasons that are not known or not understood) cannot adjust to the codes of behavior dictated by our society; therefore, they become habitual offenders. It is a saddening experience to have to accept the fact that, despite intensive training programs for counselors and supervisors instituted in a few prisons, some inmates will never be reached—even by the best-prepared behavioral scientists or others.

The prisoner is vulnerable to the possibility of many negative experiences. Too often he or she becomes the victim. Sometimes this status is forced upon the inmate; at other times it is the result of good intentions and bad results. For example, prisoners are a rich source of subjects for scientific investigations of anything from attitude change to treatment for exotic diseases:

> The drug companies, usually operating through private physicians with access to the prisons, can obtain healthy human subjects living in controlled conditions that are difficult, if not impossible, to duplicate elsewhere. In addition, the companies can buy these for a fraction—less than one-tenth, according to many medical authorities—of what they would have to pay medical students or other "free-world" volunteers. They can conduct experiments on prisoners that would not be sanctioned for student-subjects at any price because of the degree of risk and pain involved. Guidelines for human experimentation established by HEW and other agencies are easily disregarded behind prison walls.
>
> When the studies are carried out in the privacy of prison, if a volunteer becomes seriously ill, or dies, as a result of the procedures to which he is subjected, the repercussions will likely be smaller than they would be on the outside. As Rugaber discovered when trying to trace deaths resulting from the "voluntary programs," prison medical records that might prove embarrassing to the authorities have a habit of conveniently disappearing. There is minimal risk that subjects disabled by the experiments will bring lawsuits against the drug companies. Prisoners are often required to sign a waiver releasing those responsible from damage claims that may result. Such waivers have been held legally invalid as contrary to public policy and are specifically prohibited by FDA regulations, but the prisoner is unlikely to know this. The psychological effect of signing the waiver, along with the general helplessness of prisoners, makes lawsuits a rarity.[42]

In addition to sadistic, untrained guards and often uneducated and/or indifferent supervisory personnel, many prisoners (especially young inmates) are exposed to criminal sexual abuses and other physical maltreatment from fellow prisoners. In some instances young people jailed or put into prison for rather minor offenses are placed in cells with hardened, conniving, and very persuasive convicts. The danger of this forced relationship is easily determined. In other cases racial conflict is encouraged by cell assignment.

The latter indictment is very probably true, and the resultant racial clashes are certainly used to "prove" that "racial mixing" is dangerous and "unnatural" and that the races do not want to mix. It is easy to overlook personality conflict and point to "racial" causes when the individuals concerned in a disturbance are of different racial backgrounds. Little attention is paid to close interracial friendships that are formed by inmates. Often disregarded are positive relationships between minority group inmates and some supervisory personnel or even wardens. However, positive interpersonal relationships cannot develop rapidly in a climate of repression and fear.

Despite our beginning to admit that jail and prison reform is needed, the movement is too slow and too painful. In many ways we are only slightly removed from the infamous chain-gang and road-gang psychology of Georgia and other states that engaged in this inhuman practice. Fortunately there are wardens like former Warden Beto of the Texas Department of Corrections, who had the training, background, desire, and determination to bring about change and establish order in a chaotic system. Many states are now reviewing their penal codes and penal systems. Some states are permitting wives to visit and engage in sexual relationships with incarcerated husbands.

Experiments with permitting men and women prisoners to socialize is another innovation. Of course prerelease programs have proved and are proving to be very important. A dramatic drop in the rates of recidivism was found in the Texas study of its programs. Continuing studies should indicate whether or not the earlier findings remain consistent.

What happens to jail and prison populations during their periods of incarceration can have a positive or a negative effect upon these persons. It is foolish to believe that society does not or will not feel the ultimate result of the kind of treatment received by the individual who returns to the outside world. It may determine whether he is hardened and seeking revenge or, because of optimum overall conditions, has "snapped."

Again, it must be stated that efforts are being made to improve our penal system, and results are gratifying. Much of the problem rests with man's ambivalent attitude toward punishment and the kind of individual drawn to work in penal institutions. Some people are too accepting of deviant behavior; others find release of their baser emotions in this work. Society's task must be that of preparing mature, emotionally stable personnel.

CHAPTER 2

COMPLAINT
PROCEDURES

In a democratic society the legitimacy of governmental institutions and their supportive units, such as their policing agencies, is dependent upon the confidence and respect of the governed. This simple belief is particularly applicable in the area of local police forces.

The police, except in the few instances in which they actually see a crime committed, must depend on citizens to report crime, to give helpful information, to corroborate or dispute alibis, to testify in court, and to make identifications. Local police cannot function in a democracy unless they have a positive interaction with the public, or unless the citizenry accepts the policeman's role and his conduct in fulfilling that role.

Most of us have implicitly agreed to place the police in a singularly powerful position: We have armed them and tacitly sanctioned their recourse to violence. Being responsible for another individual's life is an awesome burden, and the very fact that police have assumed such a responsibility necessitates their conducting themselves in a manner above reproach.

> The fact that they represent the state does not give them immunity from the consquences of brutality or lawlessness. They, like the rioters, may be motivated by long and acute provocation. It may be that their lawlessness was the direct product of fear, or of righteous anger. They may have been moved to violence by more pressure than they could endure. But they, too, are subject to the rule of the law, and if they

exceed the authorized bounds of firmness and self-protection and needlessly assault the people whom they encounter, they should be disciplined, tried, and convicted. It is a deplorable truth that because they are officers of the state they frequently escape the penalty for their lawlessness.[1]

The chief legal sanction against illegal action by law enforcement is 18 U.S.C. 242, which prohibits officers from depriving an individual of his constitutional rights. This statute is enforced by the Justice Department's Civil Rights Division.

However, as is often the case, fact outruns theory. For example, in a review of approximately 100 files involving complaints of Mexican-Americans in the Southwest, only one example of a complete investigation was found.[2]

Similar to this criminal statute is the federal civil sanction, 42 U.S.C. 1983, which does not require proof of intent to deny one's constitutional rights. Providing for injunctions and money damages, it covers excessive force, arrest without probable cause, and other constitutional violations. Yet so few judgments were awarded under this statute that in 1961 the Civil Rights Commission concluded it to be ineffective.

Nonetheless, a workable means of policing the police is essential if they are to be the servants and not the masters of the public. A frequent source of minority hostility to police is the scarcity of effective channels for evaluating citizens' complaints against police conduct.

For example, the 1967 Civil Rights Commission Report cites inadequate investigation of complaints about the police as a primary issue in the black community. The commission even found that threats of criminal actions discouraged the filing of complaints. A Crime Commission survey adduced evidence suggesting that a lack of departmental discipline in some cities allows policemen to abuse their power with little fear of official censure.

Any system of evaluating complaints against police should be characterized by procedural fairness, both to the policeman and to the complainant, and by fair and swift disciplinary action if warranted. A thorough effort should be made to ascertain the facts of the situation, and those facts should then be publicly and honestly faced. If corrective action is necessary, the penalty imposed should be proportionate to the offense. Attempts to deny or soft-pedal official lawlessness serve only to further discredit the police and stimulate hostility, thereby making the policeman's already difficult job immeasurably more so. Former Detroit Chief of Detectives Vincent W. Piersante has cautioned his fellow

officers: ". . . We must remember that we are now in the process
of attempting to overcome the sins of commission and omission
of enforcement that for decades have been accepted as a way
of life by a minority segment of our population."[3]

Unfortunately, studies such as those undertaken by Michigan
State University and the University of California indicate that minority groups often have little faith in the police's handling of complaints against themselves.

Like most of us, policemen seldom see criticism as being
constructive. Since departments usually view complaints as an
attack on themselves, they often seek to prevent citizens from filing
grievances, thereby depriving themselves of a source of information
regarding the conduct of their jobs and further hardening minority
stereotypes of the police as the enemy.

The police are said to have several ways of discouraging
complaints. They can agree to drop criminal charges if the complainant agrees to retract his complaint or agrees not to file it.
Citizens accusing police of brutality may find themselves charged
with resisting arrest or with disorderly conduct. Alleging the filing
of a false report is another tactic used to discourage complainants.
In a large city in 1962, for instance, police arrested 16 of 41 complainants (nearly 40 percent) for filing false charges against policemen, compared to arresting 104 of 33,593 people (0.3 percent)
who filed similar charges against private citizens.[4]

Aside from such police conduct, the bureaucratic mechanics
of filing a complaint likewise tend to dissuade possible complainants. Even where a formal complaint process exists, the procedures
are often so complicated, so time-consuming, or so obscure that
the citizen abandons his efforts.

In a democratic government's relations with its citizens, the
public should possess adequate means of appealing that government's decisions and having the appeals evaluated. The channels
of appeal should be characterized by accessibility and fairness.

For example, the New York City and Oakland police departments make it known that they seek complaints, and the Chicago
Police Department keeps on record all complaints it receives. Of
course, given the corruption revealed in Fun City's finest and given
the "police riot" the Windy City police are alleged to have visited
upon people at the 1968 Democratic Convention, it is understandable if minority citizens have little faith in even the most exemplary
departments.

The mere fact that complaints must be filed with the institution allegedly having necessitated the complaint is in itself enough
to discourage minorities from initiating the process—especially in

small towns, where minority-police relations have historically been poor. Additionally, police, usually a tight-knit social group even in metropolitan areas, are even more likely to let social and personal feelings color their responses in small towns. Not surprisingly, therefore, few indictments, much less successful local prosecutions, are likely to be obtained against policemen for illegal conduct against private citizens.

Many feel the way to remedy this situation is to institute a system of internal review of police conduct. The key to the quality of internal review of citizen complaints is the commitment of the department to investigate complaints thoroughly and act accordingly. As previously noted, policemen are sensitized to the desires of their superiors and the community at large. Consequently, if ranking police officers treat complaint evaluation lightly, or treat it seriously only in time of crisis, the middle-level commanders and men on the beat will assign the complaint process a low priority.

Significantly, the aforementioned Michigan State University and California studies found that investigations conducted by the line unit involved in the allegation were frequently incomplete and unobjective, characterized by vague records and departmental regulations.

On the other hand, internal discipline consistently and firmly applied by policemen's own superiors would be more effective than externally imposed punishment because it would tend to negate the persecution syndrome many police feel when disciplined by civilians. Indeed, it could help them internalize an appropriate code of conduct, in turn enhancing their legitimacy and lessening the adversary nature of minority-police contacts.

In view of the importance of having an effective complaint evaluation process and in light of the difficulties just discussed of having an internal review system, alternative modes of evaluating complaints have been offered: court review, criminal law, and various civilian solutions.

On the whole, judicial influence on actual police conduct has been negligible, mainly because most subtle forms of police abuse, such as verbal abuse, harassment, and the like, do not actually violate criminal statutes. In cases of more blatant police excesses, such as physical abuse, there are usually few witnesses. If the alleged victim is a minority person, it is probable that the nonpolice witnesses, if any, are also minority people, or are poor, or have police records—conditions which are used to discredit their testimony. The judicial process thus seldom lessens minority-police hostility.

Significantly, many attorneys are hesitant to challenge the police because they may thereby destroy or weaken their working relationship with the police or with the district attorney. In small towns, the smaller range of contacts makes the ramifications of those contacts proportionately larger. Even in metropolitan locales, the backlog of cases and the resultant dependency of attorneys' negotiating their clients' charges and sentences increase the importance of attorney-enforcement relationships.

Of course civil damages may be obtained for physical or property injuries, medical expense, or loss of wages. Again, however, it is almost impossible to receive compensation for the subtler forms of abuse, and the same problems of credible testimony previously discussed arise. Settlements are usually small, so barristers are reluctant to act on a contingent fee basis. Finally, the expense involved in suits and a distrust of City Hall dissuade many minority people from seeking civil redress.

Much debate has centered around internal or external civilian review. Review by elected civilian officials has seldom worked because the officials lack the time, budget, or staff to properly study the complaints. Consequently, they often refer the cases to the police department, where an investigation may be qualified by any of the problems previously discussed. Again, many minority people do not trust politicians enough even to initiate the process.

Civilian review boards, once offered as a panacea, have done little but create more distrust among police and minorities. The boards have been ineffective chiefly because they lack power to decide cases or define corrective action, if any is found necessary. In fact the boards in New York City and Washington, D.C., have even been unable to give their views on a case's merits, being allowed only to recommend or not recommend a police trial.

Manpower inadequacies have further limited these boards' success. Citizens have as many procedural difficulties with civilian boards as they do with the police themselves. Slow determination of cases, improper dissemination of complaint forms, and failure to widely publicize board procedures have rendered the boards less effective than they should be.

Table 1 compares the operations of four civilian review boards.

The value of such boards remains clouded. Too frequently they become the victim of political candidates' campaign rhetoric. However, both the Michigan State and California studies found indications that the boards have had at least some success in helping redress civilian grievances against police conduct.

Until the boards transcend their advisory status, receive ade-

TABLE 1

CIVILIAN REVIEW BOARD, ORGANIZATION AND PROCEDURES

	NEW YORK	PHILADELPHIA	ROCHESTER	WASHINGTON
1. Number of members	7 (3 police)	8 (including 2 former police officers)	9	7 (2 attorneys)
2. Staff	Civilian executive director, deputy director and assistant director, 2 civilian hearing officers and staff of police officers	Full-time executive secretary	Part-time executive secretary	None
3. Jurisdiction	Any misconduct concerning community relations	Any misconduct concerning community relations	Excessive or unnecessary force	Any misconduct
4. Who may complain	Any person or group including	Victim or interested person or organization	Victim or his representative	Victim only
5. Who investigates	Board staff	Police board can also investigate	Police, but board can supplement	Police (internal investigations unit)
6. Informal settlement	Unknown	Adjustment encouraged if no "substantial physical injury"		
7. Hearing held	At discretion of board	If complainant requests unless "no cause whatsoever for citizen's complaint"	If complainant requests	At discretion of board
8. Hearings open to public	No	Yes	No	No
9. Representation by counsel allowed.	Yes	Yes	Yes	Yes

10. Counsel provided	Both sides if indigent	Indigent complainant	Indigent complainant	No
11. Evidence rules apply	No	Yes	No	Unknown
12. Cross-examination	Yes	Yes	Yes	Unknown
13. Subpoena power	Yes	No	Yes	Yes
14. Power to decide	No	No	No	No
15. Can *recommend* punishment	No, can recommend only police trial board	Yes	Yes	No, can recommend only police trial board or summary punishment
16. Recommendation made public	No parties notified	Unknown	Board's discretion	Not until Commissioners act
17. Miscellaneous	Unknown	Can recommend expunging of record	Unknown	

SOURCE: *Task Force Report: The Police*, U.S. Government Printing Office, Washington, D.C., 1967, p. 200.

quate staffing, and modify their procedures, their effectiveness will remain nominal. Even changing their advisory nature would not in itself ensure adequate evaluations. For example, New York City's all-police board has been firmer with police misconduct than Philadelphia's all-civilian board.

Yet another method of police review is appointment of an ombudsman to receive and investigate complaints regarding any government agency and bring proceedings if warranted. Ombudsmen now operate in Sweden, Finland, Denmark, Norway, New Zealand, and Great Britain, where both citizens and the government seem generally favorable to them. Because of the large scope of their jurisdiction, ombudsmen are increasingly occupied with non-police affairs.

American experience with ombudsmen has been very limited, but here too the scope of their duties is so broad as to negate their effectiveness as a police monitor. In Nassau County, New York, only 16 of 172 complaints from July 1 to December 31, 1966, concerned police conduct; only two of these had reference to police discourtesy, and none with brutality, the others dealing with traffic signals, permits, etc.[5] Perhaps, given the administrative maze in which we live, it would be wise to have ombudsmen become specialized, one dealing solely with housing complaints, one with police conduct, and so on.

In conclusion, there should exist in a democracy an adequate means for appealing the acts of government and its supportive institutions. With respect to police conduct, many citizens have this right abridged by the absence of, or the inadequacy of, complaint procedures.

While middle-class citizens are denied this check, too, minority citizens are especially victimized. Historically, minorities have stood in ignorance and awe of bureaucratic niceties, becoming prey to distrust, fear, and hostility. Today organizational complexities, the lack of procedural information, the absence of formal hearings, and the expense and confusion of court action serve to aggravate, rather than alleviate, this situation.

In its recommendations to make grievance mechanisms more effective, the Kerner Commission said the filing of a complaint should be a simple and informal process, with forms, if used, widely accessible and clearly explained. The commission also suggested that citizens be able to file complaints within their neighborhoods and with neighborhood municipal employees, rather than having to journey to a central headquarters.

The commission further recommended that a specialized agency, adequately manned and funded, deal with complaints, and that the process have an inherent conciliation system to handle complaints without requiring a complete investigation every time.

Another suggestion was that the complainant, with right to counsel, be allowed to take part in the investigation and hearings, the results of which should be made public. Furthermore, the complainant should be immediately informed of the final decision.

Finally, because many complaints concern departmental policy, not individual conduct, the policy units should be given this information and, if possible, remedial action taken in training.

The matter of complaints against police is delicate. Because the officer is vulnerable to a "frame-up," all complaints must be carefully reviewed. On the other hand, as has been noted, the civilian too is vulnerable.

Internal problems often affect the complaint procedure. In one department, even though the officer was found innocent of charges brought against him, he was never given detailed information about his case and the original complaint was never removed from his files. This situation has been corrected, but it was obvious that some officers were directing their hostility toward the complainant rather than toward a poor internal record system.

Real police professionalism will drastically reduce complaints against the officer or the department. However, nothing can substitute for a generally accepted means of assuring both the police officer and the citizen that each will receive fair and impartial treatment when charges are brought by one against the other.

Once the police assume a more professional set of internalized values, we are likely to see substantive changes in the number of instances producing complaints and an adequate evaluation process when those instances do occur.

CHAPTER 3

THE MINORITY GROUP
POLICEMAN

The Negro who enters the police role is subject to all the tensions and conflicts that arise from police work. Moreover, the conflict is compounded for the Negro: He is much more than a Negro to his ethnic group because he represents the guardian of white society, yet he is not quite a policeman to his working companions because he is stereotyped as a member of an "inferior" racial category.[1]

So far we have seen that a history of police abuse and neglect and failure to provide a meaningful grievance process have produced mutual distrust and hostility between police and minority citizens. It has been suggested that the police can change the image of their uniform by changing the color of its wearer. Hiring minorities as policemen is believed to have numerous benefits, both political and practical.

As previously noted, local police need the support of their community if they are to function properly in a democratic society. Proponents of incorporating minority citizens into police forces argue that this would reduce the stereotyping by minorities of police as goons, as well as lessen the prejudice of white policemen. Advocates stress that minorities have knowledge of the nuances of their own neighborhoods, own languages, and own subcultures seldom tapped by the average white officer.

Recruiting minorities is seen as a highly visible way of meshing the police and the community so that each might become more palatable to the other. The policeman's job would be easier, and the community would be safer. For instance, the Kerner Commission concluded the larger percentage of blacks in the Army during the Detroit riots was largely responsible for the Army's better handling of the situation than the National Guard's. A Philadelphia study found over 75 percent of the patrolmen themselves felt black policemen to be more effective in black neighborhoods than their white counterparts.[2] Minorities have an obvious advantage over white officers in surveillance and undercover work in minority communities. On such bases it is generally assumed that increased minority representation among the police would have positive results.

Despite the advantages of hiring minority officers, numerous obstacles hinder minority persons' joining the force. Culturally biased written tests and the requirement of a high school diploma effectively block many aspirants from a career in law enforcement. During the past few years, testing generally has been under serious scrutiny. The use of certain personality tests (particularly the Minnesota Multiphasic Personality Inventory) in screening for certain jobs highlighted the beginning of the questioning of the value of tests. It was conceded that some tests were useful and even very helpful in diagnosis and prognosis of a variety of conditions, but this acknowledgment did not bring an upsurge of testing. Rather, psychometricians themselves and national testing services (among them the Educational Testing Service and the Psychological Corporation) sought to correct and improve testing services.

After big business and its methods caused the surfacing of problems related to testing, education followed with some investigations. Intelligence tests and achievement tests that heretofore were widely accepted as valid and reliable instruments for a broad spectrum of educational needs found themselves gradually restricted in use and in interpretation. The question of norms became a growing issue.

The emergence of minority group consciousness is having an even greater impact upon testing. Some of the questions raised emphasize or offer new dimensions to those already being examined for the larger (basically white) population. Other, more serious evaluations are minority-group specific. For example, the language problem that may influence scores on tests given to individuals for whom English is not the basic language is now being appraised. Cultural factors that may affect scores are receiving marked attention.

More interesting is the fact that minority group professionals are becoming involved and are being sought as test developers and consultants. In the past, their expertise remained untapped because of the employment practices of our society, which severely limited vocational opportunity and the development of highly diversified minority employment pools.

National concern has been aroused recently about testing and the use of minorities in education and employment. For example, participants at the National Conference on Minority Group Testing in Education and Employment held at Hampton Institute, Hampton, Virginia, April 1–4, 1973, pointed up the adverse effects that testing may be having upon minority group recruiting and hiring among various industries and agencies. This was not to say that tests should not be used in screening minority group applicants or evaluating them for promotion, but in too many instances such tests, not assessed for cultural or linguistic bias, may have resulted in false negatives.

As an aside, the testing problem is often seen by minorities as suited to the desires of bigoted law enforcement officials. They would be well within the law on the grounds of departmental regulations, while keeping larger numbers of blacks and Mexican-Americans off the force, by using biased evaluation procedures.

Some departments have made efforts to resolve this problem. The Albany, New York, Civil Service Board, though it already employs professionals in its testing program, has reviewed evaluation procedures for the selection of police officers in order to eliminate subtle barriers to minority hiring. The implementing of suggestions is the most important aspect of a manifested concern. Many departments are willing to follow through to the suggestion phase but then fail to implement. Funds for completing these projects could save much of the money spent on armament necessary to fight the symptoms of incomplete programs of evaluation and implementation in screening and promotional procedures.

It is generally agreed that at least a high school diploma should be a prerequisite for law enforcement work. In fact, some suggest at least a junior college education with special emphasis on the social sciences (aspects of human behavior). The law enforcement elements are best handled in academies or in specially designed programs of law enforcement being offered by many colleges (e.g., Sam Houston State College, Huntsville, Texas, and Howard University, Washington, D.C.).

However, there may be elements of police work that would permit a less than high school background. This possibility should be determined by the department along with experts in the area. It might motivate a good candidate to pass his G.E.D., get a high school equivalency diploma, and enter formal training as a police cadet.

There are several other possibilities for motivating excellent prospects who lack the educational background. For minority groups, the carrot has so long been dangled that they have no faith. Usually, they must see opportunity before they become excited about achieving. By having no program to meet the motivation or achievement needs of some individuals, law enforcement may be automatically eliminating likely candidates for law enforcement training.

Unfortunately, the recruitment officer seldom points out the many and varied jobs available in law enforcement. Generally one sees only the police officer. What about the technicians? What about the instructional staff? These are only two possibilities. Indeed, well-trained technicians may decide to become officers after having seen that law enforcement is much more than apprehending and arresting criminals. The research opportunities are rarely presented. How many scientists ignore the field who might otherwise be interested and have much to offer? The seeming closed-mindedness about behavioral scientists has shut out very important jobs. Psychologists and others might well be turned on to jobs as police officers who could serve several functions, including the obviously missing mental health and research functions.

To recruit successfully, law enforcement must paint a much broader picture than that of a black police officer smiling at a black child or arresting a black criminal. The color of a man's skin does not guarantee anything. Certainly, the employment of minorities is important, but the first requirement is to recruit desirable candidates regardless of color or ethnicity. The Mexican-American or black officer can represent "more of the same in living color" if recruitment and screening procedures do not keep pace with the changing times.

Many Mexican-Americans are denied police jobs because little or no effort is made to bridge the language gap, and because police departments often maintain strict height qualifications. Years of improper nutrition and inadequate medical care may make it difficult for many Mexican-Americans to pass rigid physical exams, and what may be a culturally defined height problem aggravates the situation.

A lesser minority recruitment problem is related to criminal records. It is no secret that discrimination generally exists in the prosecution and sentencing of blacks. Our current concern is how this practice affects minority group recruitment.

Minority group persons are often prevented from entering

police work because they have a police record, regardless of the overall circumstances. It is a fact in America that a minority group person is more likely to have a police record than a white person. The social upheavals of the middle 1960s greatly increased that likelihood. Individuals and groups lamented the harsh sentences given blacks for civil rights activities—especially when it was obvious that the acts were for "inciting to riot" or "loitering," although in numerous instances facts did not justify even the arrest. While many of these persons were later released and harsh sentences designed to discourage protest were mitigated, a number of excellent candidates may be denied an opportunity to become law enforcement officers now because they have a record. During this restless period in our history it cannot be denied that activists often were charged with felonies for behaviors and acts that would more appropriately have been defined as misdemeanors.

Blacks and other minorities are also adversely affected by pay and status. Police pay is so low that most individuals who can meet the requisites can get, and want, better jobs. A history of police discrimination in promotions and general status may discourage persons from applying.

> Past discrimination or even the belief that discrimination
> does or has existed has much the same effect as actual,
> present discrimination.[3]

It is not surprising then to find minorities, in proportion to their percentage of the population, underrepresented on police rosters (see Table 2).

The figures in Table 2 represent the racial compositions of the entire departments. The percentages of minority citizens in supervisory positions within these departments are even lower. Thus, still another factor dissuading minorities from seeking police careers is difficulty in advancing, whether working in or outside the South. Following is the ratio of white supervisory officers to white officers generally, and black supervisory officers to black officers generally, in the southern and border state cities.[4]

	Sergeants	Lieutenants	Captains
White	1:8	1:20	1:37
Negro	1:16	1:125	1:246

The situation is no better in the North. Here are the corresponding ratios for the northern cities surveyed.[5]

	Sergeants	Lieutenants	Captains
White	1:9	1:25	1:45
Negro	1:20	1:108	1:311

TABLE 2

PERCENT NONWHITE POLICE AND PERCENT NONWHITE POPULATION OF SOME MAJOR CITIES

NAME OF DEPT.	% NON-WHITE POP.	% NON-WHITE POLICE OFFICERS	RATIO: SERG. TO OFFICERS		RATIO: LIEUT. TO OFFICERS		RATIO: CAPT. TO OFFICERS		RATIO: ABOVE CAPT. TO OFFICERS	
			N.W.	W.	N.W.	W.	N.W.	W.	N.W.	W.
Atlanta, Ga.	38*	10	1:49	1:73	1:33	1:16	0:98	1:58	0:98	1:145
Baltimore, Md.	41*	7	1:30	1:7	1:69	1:27	1:208	1:167	1:208	1:135
Boston, Mass.	11*	2	1:49	1:11	0:49	1:31	0:49	1:123	0:49	1:205
Buffalo, N.Y.	18*	3	1:37	1:22	1:37	1:11	0:37	1:56	0:37	1:42
Chicago, Ill.	27*	17	1:21	1:9	1:921	1:35	1:1842	1:127	1:307	1:140
Cincinnati, Ohio	28*	6	1:27	1:12	1:27	1:25	0:54	1:64	0:54	1:120
Cleveland, Ohio	34*	7	1:28	1:13	1:165	1:26	0:165	1:79	0:165	1:121
Dayton, Ohio	26*	4	1:16	1:7	0:16	1:30	0:16	1:67	0:16	1:100
Detroit, Mich.	39*	5	1:25	1:12	1:114	1:26	No such rank		1:227	1:66
Hartford, Conn.	20*	11	1:38	1:10	1:38	1:20	0:38	1:34	0:38	1:152
Kansas City, Mo.	20*	6	1:7	1:6	0:51	1:24	0:51	1:80	1:51	1:63
Louisville, Ky.	21*	6	1:35	1:13	1:35	1:18	0:35	1:53	1:35	1:75
Memphis, Tenn.	38*	5	No such rank		1:12	1:4	0:46	1:18	0:46	1:19
Mich. St. Pol.	9***	a¹	0:1	1:11	0:1	1:63	0:1	1:79	0:1	1:500
New Haven, Conn.	19**	7	0:31	1:21	0:31	1:26	0:31	1:35	0:31	1:69
New Orleans, La.	41*	4	1:8	1:12	1:54	1:25	0:54	1:46	0:54	1:125
New York, N.Y.	16*	5	1:23	1:15	1:74	1:28	1:743	1:96	1:495	1:116
New Jersey St. Pol.	9***	a¹	0:5	1:7	0:5	1:28	0:5	1:72	0:5	1:305
Newark, N.J.	40*	10	1:37	1:17	1:61	1:18	1:184	1:77	None listed	
Oakland, Calif.	31*	4	1:27	1:7	0:27	1:25	1:27	1:63	0:27	1:210
Oklahoma City, Okla.	15*	4	0:16	1:13	1:16	1:22	0:16	1:38	0:16	1:70
Philadelphia, Pa.	29*	20	1:53	1:18	1:172	1:40	1:459	1:120	0:1377	1:240
Phoenix, Ariz.	8*	1	0:7	1:8	1:7	1:32	0:7	1:70	0:7	1:175
Pittsburgh, Pa.	19*	7	1:36	1:11	1:36	1:31	0:109	1:362	1:109	1:242
St. Louis, Mo.	37*	11	1:11	1:9	1:75	1:40	1:56	1:107	0:224	1:165
San Francisco, Calif.	14*	6	0:102	1:8	0:102	1:25	0:102	1:110	0:102	1:165
Tampa, Fla.	17*	3	0:17	1:10	0:17	1:41	0:17	1:38	0:17	1:62
Washington, D.C.	63*	21	1:29	1:10	1:186	1:20	1:186	1:58	0:559	1:70

SOURCE: *Task Force Report: The Police*, p. 195, citing National Capital Area Civil Liberties Union, "A Proposed Revision of the System for Processing Complaints Against Police Misconduct in the District of Columbia," January 1964.

a¹ Less than ½ of 1%.

* % Negro population figures, 1965 estimates by the Center for Research in Marketing, *Cong. Quarterly*, Weekly Report, No. 36, Sept. 8, 1967.

** % Negro population figures, 1966 estimates, Office of Economic Opportunity.

*** % Negro population figures for states of Michigan and New Jersey, 1960 Census Figures.

The Kerner Commission found that in every instance where statistics were available blacks were, relative to population, underrepresented.

Mexican-Americans face a comparable situation. In 243 police departments studied in the Southwest, 5.7 percent of the total (uniformed, plainclothes, and civilian) personnel were Mexican-American, compared to their 11.8 percent of the population.[6] Of 23,944 uniformed officers, 5.2 percent were Mexican-American.[7]

Given these statistics alone, it is understandable why a minority group person might not choose law enforcement as a profession. Most officers indicate that some police departments vigorously recruit minorities but, once they are accepted and commissioned, show little or no concern for their opportunities to advance. In fact, encouragement is usually totally lacking. Where it is given, the discriminatory aspects of the hurdles to be cleared are overlooked, or (at least unconsciously) they are expected to be super-blacks or super-Mexican-Americans.

No attempt is made to equalize their opportunities for promotion. When questioned about this, the average command officer blandly replies, "They just don't seem to be able to pass the exams." In Houston, it was interesting that black college graduates (from highly reputable schools) could not "qualify" as lieutenants, captains, etc., when white police who had a not too exciting high school record advanced to these positions over their obviously better-educated colleagues. The situation was not sufficiently embarrassing to the force to be carefully examined. Of course, this example can be extended to numerous police departments. Blacks feel forced into a "super" position just to be "equal" to an academically and often intellectually inferior white officer.

Minority police officers often find themselves on the hardest beats, in high-crime areas. The rationale may be understandable but what escapes the minority group officer's comprehension is the lack of compensatory consideration given him. He feels it unfair that he is expected to function well here and produce in a manner equal to that of his fellow officer who has a less difficult assignment, in fact or in psychological terms.

Getting hired and getting promoted are only two of a minority policeman's concerns. Acceptance by his fellow officers is a huge hurdle. The problem of acceptance is insidious and dual in nature. The second part of it is related to his acceptance by the black community—the latter being less insidious but more frustrating. Like most minority groups, police feel that no one can understand them so they must close ranks for mutual support. Usually the minority group officer is included here but out of necessity rather than with the openness and warmth given the white officer. Both white and black officers have admitted this discrepancy but see it as a possible carry-over from the larger society.

It appears that the bigotry of a few officers can influence the majority of the other officers. In many departments, black officers indicate their belief that bigotry is so much a way of life that officers who tend not to be racist actually don't see the acts of racism around them. When this possibility was presented to an administrative officer in one large southwestern metropolitan police force, he decided to see for himself.

He recounted his experience in terms similar to these: "I went into the coffee shop and looked around at the officers who were taking a break. I noticed two black officers at a table and particularly was I aware of the fact that they were sitting alone. No white officer had joined them despite the fact that a large number of white officers were in the coffee shop. I decided that I would join them. When I went over and sat down, a look of utter surprise came over their faces. This shock was readily apparent in spite of the fact that I knew both of them and we liked each other. I could not help being aware of the glances and even gazes of some of the white officers who were having coffee or just taking a break. Some appeared to reflect surprise; others seemed to show resentment. I had never been aware of this before. This was my first experience of the kind of loneliness that black officers must feel on some police forces. I made up my mind from that point on that I would make it a point to drink coffee or take breaks with the black and Mexican-American officers on our force. I hoped that this example would carry over to some of the other officers who I am sure would like to do so but who fear doing so for one reason or the other. I will never forget the feeling that I had, and I will always be grateful for having been awakened to something that I had not realized was going on."

There are many subtle ways in which minority group police are kept out of law enforcement agencies. One white officer from a state partol, for example, volunteered the following. He was made acutely aware of subtle means of discriminating, he said, when he heard a top administrative officer say, to a well-qualified prospective black candidate, something to this effect: "We welcome you here and we want you to be a part of our state highway patrol. We are glad to have you but I think it my responsibility to point out a few of the problems that you may face. One, of course, is that of your stopping a white woman on the highway. You may be alone and if, of course, she screams or brings some charge against you I am not sure how it will turn out. After all, she will be white, she will be a woman; and you will be black. Naturally the department will want to assist you in any way possible but we would have to go over and over the facts and, although it may be unfair, it is highly likely that the word of the woman would be accepted over yours. I don't want to discourage you; but I think it is only fair that you know what you may be up against."

Further, the administrative officer also indicated to the candidate the loneliness he might feel as a member of a minority group in an overwhelmingly white situation. He could not assure him that he would be accepted by the other officers and commented that he would have little control over how he was treated. Nevertheless, he was sure that with the record the candidate was bringing in he would be able to handle the situation. He suggested that the new officer try to avoid trouble and if he was confronted by bigoted officers remember that he might be a kind of Jackie Robinson on the state highway patrol. Nothing was ever said about how he might be protected by the organization. It seemed that he was expected to take whatever came from fellow officers or the general public without flinching, without argument, without resistance, and without complaining.

At the time the individual was recounting this story there appeared to be only two or three blacks in the agency, and they were assigned desk jobs rather than regular patrol functions. There is no record of how many times this episode has been repeated in highway patrol situations or in police situations. It reveals a technique that may be used in many agencies, to discourage minority group recruits while at the same time appearing to welcome them and to be "fair" with them regarding what they may expect. Such tactics seem to be subsiding, and one sees an increasing number of blacks on highway patrols. However, the states that have few or no blacks or Mexican-Americans remain highly suspect in the minds of minorities.

There are countless ways to discriminate within departments and yet be within the law, to harass without the victim's being able to define the behavior as harassment, to demean without its being apparent that the behavior was intended to demean. When such negative conduct is prevalent, those officers who resent it are unlikely to say anything. Rather, some admit that they may be influenced to join the crowd in order to avoid peer pressure.

It is extremely difficult to be in this kind of no-man's-land. It must be almost impossible to function in a situation in which one feels not totally accepted but can say little about the problem. At the same time, admitting to being a part of a society that is closed to the general public and largely closed to oneself exerts great psychological pressure. To function at maximum efficiency must seem a herculean task when superimposed upon all of the usual problems, frustrations, and dangers faced by the average officer are those frustrations and that pain suffered by virtue of being a minority group member.

Most black officers point to full and equal acceptance by a very disappointingly small number of their peers. Thus the loneliness felt as a result of the ratio of blacks to whites increases. When they see what they perceive as racist acts on the part of fellow officers and feel themselves the victims of these practices, bitterness and impotent anger are aroused because of fear of verbalizing feelings or openly pointing to the acts. Usually they display little or no emotion and salve their hurt by saying that being on the force may help or that in time they will "overcome." To many blacks and Mexican-Americans it isn't worth it.

Most whites must sense, and most minorities know, that the true feelings of blacks and Mexican-Americans are not always openly displayed. What they say may not be interpreted the same way by whites and the minority community. For their own protection minorities have long been able to communicate in ways almost incomprehensible to white Americans. Most black officers conceal their feelings when white police are reluctant to report acts of racism by their peers, when command officers tend to overlook such behavior, when chiefs of police refuse to punish or relieve racist officers of their duties or discharge them from the force, and when they have (except in a few departments) little chance for equal acceptance and treatment.

Several white officers who wanted to work with black partners reported (1) rigorous questioning by command officers, (2) technical reasons for refusing the request, (3) subtle acts to discourage the continuation of relationships, (4) open refusal, and (5) an O.K. with a warning. Of course, this is not always the case. There are interracial pairs of police officers who are inseparable. Color does not enter the relationship, and respect is mutual. The white officers of such teams tend to be exceptional men who refuse to be intimidated by the possibility of being socially ostracized or quietly criticized. The number of courageous white officers is increasing, as is the total acceptance of minority group officers. This is, indeed, a good and healthy sign.

Lack of acceptance by the black and brown community is a deterrent to black and brown prospects but in no way compares to the deterring factors found within law enforcement agencies. However, a minority policeman does risk ostracism by his own neighborhood, which may consider him a "Tom" or "Tio." He becomes a minority within another minority, neither of which is liked by his fellows.

Police, like soldiers, often simplify their job by objectifying their targets; it's far easier to bust a label than a personal acquaintance. Because minority police are more likely than white police to know their suspect, the violator, or the person across a confrontation line, they walk a singluar sort of psychological tightrope.

> No one can hurt you unless he is your friend. And you won't
> let people become your friends.[8]
>
>   . . .
>
> And at the same time you have to enforce laws on the demon-
> strators and during these times your heart beats out for them.
> You have a dual feeling. Especially if you are assigned in
> front of a school and you know in your heart that the situation
> exists, because you went to these schools.[9]

In his study of black policemen, Nicholas Alex concluded that blacks choose police work because of the scarcity of alternatives and because civil service jobs are steady and relatively well-paying occupations. Thus, some blacks seek police careers, not because of the pull of the attraction of being a policeman, but because of the push of economic and employment conditions.

Historically, law enforcement has offered white immigrants an avenue to economic and social prestige, however limited. Since the have-nots have now become the haves, it is said, they resent what they consider intrusion by minorities seeking to repeat the process. Sometimes this resentment is interpreted as bigotry rather than a reaction to threat.

The solutions to the problem of minority participation in law enforcement are implicit in the problem itself. Increased minority participation in police work will occur when less emphasis is given "white" qualifying examinations, when allowances are made for juvenile and adolescent records, when psychological tests are designed to prevent bigoted malcontents from becoming policemen, when frivolous qualifications such as height stipulations are abandoned, and when pay becomes proportionate to the responsibilities.

A bad police image can't be improved overnight, but nominal steps can be taken. For example, more programs can be developed in which applicants are given general education courses to help them pass high school equivalency tests, and then receive special training. Those below the minimum requisite ages at the program's end may enter the department's regular cadet program or accept temporary civilian jobs within the department. Applicants can be taught clerical skills which they can use within the force or in nonpolice work if they are rejected eventually as police officers. However, if an applicant has to satisfy the regular standards of the department before being admitted to the program, that provision can negate the effects of an otherwise promising approach.[10]

Concern with hiring minority policemen assumes that a bettering of police-minority relations will follow. This assumption is open to debate. The aforementioned California study found that blacks in San Diego and Philadelphia frequently believed black officers to be harsher than their white counterparts. In some instances low-income citizens have preferred white officers because of the severity of black police.

In another previously cited study of police brutality, it was found that 67 percent of the citizens victimized by white officers were white and 71 percent of those victimized by black police were black.[11] Police seem prone to exercise force against their own race. Even in the darkest days of the White South, white police probably used quantitatively more force against whites because social lines were so rigid and the penalty for crossing the lines was so cruel and so well known that blacks, or browns, seldom crossed them. It must no longer be assumed that solving the color problem will solve the overall image problem of law enforcement.

In conclusion, we may say that hiring minority citizens as law enforcement officers is thought to have definite advantages: improving police-community relations, correcting proportionate underrepresentation in large cities, and simplifying the policeman's job in volatile neighborhoods. What is required is the elimination of superficial standards and the professionalization of recruiting and training methods. At first glance the problem is relatively simple—and soluble. However, the issues are essentially deeper than eliminating racial and ethnic barriers to equal opportunity. We are actually considering questions of how we are to govern ourselves and each other.

The questions we have so far discussed—police abuse and neglect, the inadequacy of grievance mechanisms, and now the employment and promotion of minority officers—seem to require national, not merely local, commitments. Professionalization implies uniformity and centralization.

Yet American law enforcement has historically been a local responsibility. And many people, from John Birchers to Black Panthers, want law enforcement to remain in the local domain. The assumption of local accountability for police work largely explains the great variety in the quality of police departments. If justice is to be indivisible, police reform may have to be national.

Furthermore, we should ask ourselves whether simply employing and promoting minority officers constitutes a change of substance or mere form. As noted, there is evidence that minority police use more force than white officers against minority citizens. Color in and of itself does not guarantee professional police practices, and to concentrate on color compositions of police forces ignores the more central questions of hiring and training practices.

Likewise, the concern with minority promotions may be self-defeating. A policeman has more chance to positively affect his community on the beat, not in an air-conditioned office in City Hall. Too often responsible, compassionate officers are promoted to supervisory roles or placed in "community-relations centers" where they give coloring books to children. Meanwhile, a less sensitized officer may be dealing with the community on a daily basis. When promotions remove responsible policemen from the human sphere of action, the policy is counterproductive.

Obviously the problem of the minorities in police work can have its paradoxes. This need not be the case if in recruiting no "lowering of standards" is implied and hiring practices are aimed at more than just increasing the number of minorities. Action in this area must not be precipitous. It must be honest, careful, and deliberate. Above all it must be fair. All of this suggests meticulous evaluation and manifest commitment with all of its concomitants.

Finally, the minority group policeman must be seen first as a law enforcement officer. His difference must be accepted as an asset when it is acutally that, but as only an accident of birth at other times. The white law enforcement officer must be seen by minorities as abiding fully by the laws (especially laws related to constitutional guarantees of equal opportunity and equal treatment) if the profession is to attract desirable, law-abiding members of oppressed groups.

Recruitment of minorities for the profession of law enforcement need not be troublesome. The ease or difficulty in recruiting relates directly to the degree of honesty and commitment of the agency involved—no more, no less.

Recruitment of minorities for the profession of law enforcement will be greatly facilitated when all Americans, but more especially law enforcement agencies, admit the obstacles that they themselves place in front of the minority group individual who may be fully qualified to be a police officer. Once that admission is made, it should be a much easier job to eliminate both real and imagined illegal and immoral barriers.

White law enforcement must become increasingly aware of the psychological pain suffered by black officials who want desperately to be accepted as highly professional officers, but who feel unaccepted as fraternal brothers.

Americans tend to deny or not to see the extra burdens, the extra frustrations, the subtle discriminatory practices experienced by blacks in various professions. The police profession cannot afford this attitude. The mental health of a black or Mexican-American officer is just as important as that of a white officer. It is unfair to have extra expectations of the black officer, who already feels generally that he must be "super" in order to be accepted. When equal acceptance and equal treatment are realities for minority group individuals, there will be no problem of recruitment to the profession of law enforcement. "The problem of discrimination in law enforcement is only a problem to white police officers to the extent that they have internalized the code of the impersonal nondiscriminatory rule of law."[12]

Fortunately, efforts to achieve these ends are being felt across the country. Much of the responsibility now belongs to the black and the Mexican-American. They must take advantage of the new opportunities. It is their additional responsibility openly to resist discriminatory practices when they occur and to work within the system to effect real and lasting change. No one else can do it for the member of a minority group. It may still be difficult, but he will now have more individuals willing to assist him. The reward certainly will be worth the effort. It may in fact point the way to a more equitable system of justice.

PART TWO

THE COURTS

INTRODUCTION TO PART TWO

In a society ostensibly ruled by law, the ultimate institutional safe-guard against official tyranny is the judicial system. The courts are seen as the seat of justice, whether federal, state, or local. Here passions are moderated; facts are presented; a jury of peers decides upon a verdict based upon conclusive and indisputable evidence; a judge, in his or her infinite wisdom, passes sentence or otherwise disposes of the case according to law.

Most of us fail to realize the pervasive influence the courts exert upon our lives. Although our direct involvement in the judicial process may be minimal, courts can affect us by substantially shaping the climate in which we live.

. . . If people—their lives, their futures, and their attitudes toward law—are the heartblood of the criminal process, then

the local municipal court must fulfill the needs and expectations which focus not on conviction or acquittal, or getting
off on a technicality, but on fair and speedy treatment and
representation by a trustworthy advocate.[1]

The constantly embattled Supreme Court is direct evidence of court
decision versus people and people versus court decision in a struggle to have laws interpreted in an acceptable and equitable manner
for all concerned citizens.

As a means of appealing governmental or individual abuses,
the judicial process can represent an essential protector or an
omnipotent enemy. The courts are not without problems because
courts are people and people are not perfect. In addition, the courts
mirror the moods and concerns of their many publics. They can
also reflect public apathy.

Part Two does not claim to be an exhaustive examination
and discussion of the judiciary system. A rather substantial body
of literature (from which we shall quote) more adequately covers
this subject. Our aim is to introduce to some people, and remind
others of, the important functions of the court system.

Further, Part Two attempts in simple terms to present the
view of this process from the vantage point of the lay individual
who may not have the sophistication of a legal mind and who
seeks answers to calm his fears of legal proceedings or to undergird
his faith in the legal process. The endeavor in this part is to say,
"Here are the weaknesses that we see and the criticisms made
by others, but couched in simple, straightforward terms. What
is being done to *ensure* liberty and justice for all—the minorities,
the handicapped, the poor? Do courts mete out judgments in an
impartial and equitable manner regardless of race, color, religion,
ethnicity, and sex? If not, how can our system of checks and balances rectify the situation?"

Representation by counsel and jury participation are crucial
to a fair trial. However, for some individuals (and especially for
members of minority groups) their legal defense may consist of
underrepresentation or misrepresentation by counsel and the exclusion of peers from the jury—particularly blacks and Mexican-
Americans. The problem of exclusion of blacks and Mexican-Americans from juries may be diminishing, but where? How fast? Poor
counsel and jury exclusion make a mockery of the entire democratic
process and erode a philosophically sound system of justice.

Claims of discriminatory jail sentences and unfair bail bond
procedures also haunt the judicial process. Discriminatory jail sentences and alienation from full participation in the judicial process

is not new to the Afro-American, the Mexican-American, and the economically disadvantaged white citizen. The following is a Texas news release of March 15, 1974:

The Chicano is alienated from participation in the legal system today because he has seen that system manifest an inability to deal effectively with the problems of the poor, Judge Carlow Cadena of the Court of Civil Appeals in San Antonio said Friday (March 15) at the University of Texas School of Law.

Speaking at a symposium on the Chicano and the Legal System sponsored by the Law School and the Chicano Law Students Association, Judge Cadena outlined the reasons he feels the Chicano community is at best indifferent and at worst hostile to the present system of laws and law enforcement.

"Today, respect for the system of administration of justice is at a low ebb," Judge Cadena said. "Minority groups see what causes the rest of the population to have so little respect, but they see these defects, such as disparity in sentencing, as peculiarly affecting them."

Judge Cadena cited the case of a Houston policeman who was given two years' probation for pleading guilty to possession of 76 pounds of marijuana while a San Antonio youth was given 25 years in jail for possession of 16 marijuana cigarettes.

He said the legal system has failed to help solve the problems of the poor, of whom Chicanos make up a large portion, because of the traditional training and concept of the role of the lawyer.

While not discounting the importance of the test case and the neighborhood law office in dealing with Chicano legal problems, Judge Cadena said public serving lawyers must learn to educate the poor about their rights and in some cases help them organize to bring the kind of "political and economic pressure which other groups successfully and without much condemnation frequently exert."

The pro bono lawyer has lost sight of the fact that effective change for the long term can best be brought about not in the courts but in the legislature and in business circles, he said.

The Chicano is also alienated simply by virtue of the fact that he is a Chicano, Judge Cadena said and added:

"Many Mexicanos don't feel at ease if they have to talk to an Anglo lawyer about their problems."

"The Chicano remembers his recent past," Judge Cadena said. He knows that in many places Mexican-American children could not go to "white" schools, that until recently he was considered unfit to sit on a grand jury and that even today it may be difficult for him to move into a fairly good neighborhood. Even when he's finally admitted to sit on a board or serve on a grand jury, he knows that it is "for show-case effect. There is some degree of humiliation to know you're sitting on a board or grand jury because someone felt obligated."

Judge Cadena urged Chicano students to remember "you are going to fail at some things because you just don't have it. Not every Chicano is a genius, or can be a good accountant, or can graduate from law school even if he is admitted. Don't use the existence of these problems as a crutch or an excuse.[2]

The bail bond business is an important cog in the wheel of justice, but it often benefits the hardened criminal and punishes the lesser offender. Unscrupulous individuals can harm any legitimate business enterprise. In the case of the unprofessional and unprincipled bail bondsmen, the result of his behavior can echo endlessly and destructively down the corridors of justice.

Perhaps the chapters in Part Two will tweak the conscience of those directly involved in service to the indicted so as to assure endeavors toward equity and impartiality. It is hoped that Part Two will arouse readers to their duty and responsibility in an area that too often we leave entirely to others, feeling that we have no part in a system that sets our standards of behavior and punishes us for deviant conduct.

CHAPTER 4

THE
CURTAILED
COURTS

A democratic form of government, through constituted authority, guarantees certain rights to the individual. The Fourteenth Amendment (1868) to the Constitution of the United States of America states: ". . . Nor shall any state deprive any person of life, liberty or property, without due process of law; nor deny to any person within its jurisdiction the equal protection of the laws." In order to accomplish this aim, the adversary system of law was established, with its rather elaborate scheme of checks and balances. Unfortunately, this system, designed to protect the rights of the individual, is so complex that it becomes awesome to many persons and tends to alienate and frighten others. Thus the very machinery that was meant to serve the legal needs of the individual in reality often works in a manner contrary to its purpose.

Of the numerous reasons for this state of affairs, possibly one of the most prevalent, yet the least obvious, is the degree of ignorance among the general public about the nature and function of our court system. It might be interesting to determine the number of Americans who know that they have what is called a dual court system, which "may have some advantages but which exacts a high price in terms of time, money, and efficiency."[1] Although most people are aware that there are state courts and federal courts, probably few understand the jurisdiction or the mandate of these courts. Unless an individual has reason to be exposed to the court system, he is generally unfamiliar with the various kinds of courts, their locations, their hierachical arrangements, and the discretionary procedures within the judiciary sys-

tem. Kerper's *Introduction to the Criminal Justice System* discusses
the criminal justice process in a very lucid and meaningful way.
Although designed for maximum protection of individual rights,
court proceedings, which are complex and often complicated, can
expose the individual to misfirings of justice simply because he
lacks sophistication in the area. Our legal process makes available
lawyers versed in the intricacies of court procedure, but it is a
documented fact that the more the *individual* knows about and
understands court procedure, the greater will be his opportunity
to fully utilize the law.

Minorities and the poor are especially vulnerable to acts of
injustice because they do not readily have access to information
about their rights under the law or know how the courts are designed to function in order to assure those rights. Even with counsel, minorities and the poor are likely to be denied full protection
under the law despite the "due process" specifically conceived to
guarantee that protection.

Ralph Nader, for example, has noted the inequity of a legal
process "designed largely for the powerful to contend among themselves or against the weak."

Every profession has its own myths, totems, and taboos. In
the legal profession these serve to camouflage the dependency
of the legal status quo on the established power systems.
To begin with, most Americans cannot use the legal system
for the vast majority of their grievances. These grievances
individually represent causes of small dollar amount or important quests for rights which are not dollar-structured. Retainer
astigmatism being what it is, lawyers in the aggregate are
uninterested in most of these potential clients. Judicial and
administrative politics, archaic-authoritarian procedures, and
endemic delays comprise an additional layer of obstacles to
the use of the law. Finally, civil rights, poverty rights, consumer rights, environmental rights, and procedural rights are
expected to be defended by single or small-group parties who
cannot afford the costs of the legal system. As a result, the
paradox of a wealth of abuse (consumer fraud, for example)
and a poverty of access by individual victims grows more
acute as society grows increasingly complex.

·   ·   ·

Rights were confused with both the availability of remedies
and the ability to endure the attrition necessary to secure
such rights.

In a rawer dimension, most lawyers have not been distressed
at all to have the law define violence in such a way as to
exclude most of the large-scale violence from the embrace
of the law. Environmental pollution, mass malnutrition, rotting
tenements, defectively designed or constructed consumer
products, and job injuries and diseases are major forms of
violence. Yet the law has remained mostly silent as the destruction of people's property, health, and safety has continued
to climb and as new risks to unborn generations accumulate.[2]

Individuals who suffer from the kinds of violence mentioned
by Nader—pollution, malnutrition, rotting tenements, and the
like—tend to be minorities and the poor. These groups exhaust
most of their energies in an effort just to survive. Consequently
there is little time for them to be concerned about learning legal
niceties that can be used in a court to ameliorate their situation.
In fact, most of them don't even know their rights. Where city
governments have attempted to make certain that their citizens
knew and understood their rights, it has been done in a rather
academic way. That is to say, some city governments published
materials and mailed them out with the expectation that all citizens
would receive the information and thereby become informed of
the services available to them and the protection guaranteed by
their local governing body.

The intent of this effort is laudable, but its overall success
has not been adequately evaluated—particularly as regards the
groups most in need of information explaining their rights and
how they might be assured of obtaining those rights. Disadvantaged individuals are so accustomed to discrimination that they
are not likely to feel included in any show of concern by local
government for its citizens. Consequently, minorities and the poor
ordinarily ignore any material distributed by city government—
especially that related to services or protection. In addition to for-
feiting many of their rights because of a credibility gap between
city government and this segment of the citizenry, a sizable number
of these individuals lack the ability to read and comprehend the
information.

In some instances representatives from local poverty agencies
and VISTA workers have attempted to help the poor secure their
rights by initiating court actions. In what would seem to be a
paradox, some of the cities that went to the expense of printing
and distributing information designed to help the citizen assure
himself of certain rights labeled these workers "troublemakers."
Other city governments demanded that VISTA workers be moved

out of their cities or that their activities related to helping the poor develop suits be stopped. Whether or not local governments were justified in their sometimes frantic and massive efforts to prevent legal action by minorities and the poor, the end result seems to have been the hampering of justice. Thus the ability of the courts to assure justice may be curtailed by ignorance of the law, ignorance of court function, or the outright blocking of the path to justice for a given segment of society.

One of the most universally accepted problems of the courts is that of the crowded docket. The case loads in some courts are so great that one senses a stifling of the entire judicial process. The problem of having too few courts and too few judges can only mean situations that are unfair to all concerned. It is not possible to give studied attention to the details of each case under these circumstances. Both the plaintiff and the defendant are exposed to the possibility of judgment by whim, fatigue, time-press, emotion, or other externally induced pressures, rather than opinion based on a careful consideration of all the facts.

An increase in the number of cases brought before a judge hinders attempts to deliver prompt and fair decisions. Chief Justice Warren Burger, for example, cites the following figures:

> From 1940 to 1970:
> – Personal injury cases multiplied 5 times
> – Petitions from state prisoners seeking federal habeas
>   corpus relief increased from 89 to over 12,000
> – During this period Congress increased the number of
>   judges by 70%, while the total number of cases filed
>   in the federal district courts nearly doubled.[3]

These large case loads can have a definite effect on the manner of their disposition.

> For example, the only available alternatives for handling the 75 thousand drunk cases yearly are a penal sentence, commitment to one understaffed, overcrowded alcoholism treatment center, or complete release without supervision. And when probation is used, the individual probation officers have such large caseloads that they can do little more than talk to their probationers occasionally on the phone. All too frequently, the probation officer's invitation to "come in and talk" turns out to mean "come in and wait an hour for me to finish in court." Even the most patient and concerned judge or probation officer is subject to the financial whims of legislature

and local communities which fail to establish and fund rehabilitation programs with adequate staff and facilities.[4]

Although this example is related to cases involving inordinate
drinking, analogies may be drawn concerning other kinds of cases.
A most encouraging move was made by a judge in Texas who
decided to do something about the case-load problem. When she
subpoenaed a large number of police officers and required that
they fulfill their responsibility to the court in cases involving them,
she drew quick ire from city officials. However, the result of her
actions was so beneficial and so meaningful that criticism immediately turned to praise. It is refreshing to see courage, intellectual
honesty, and a sincere concern for the citizen exemplified by impeccable judicial discretion.

Law reacts to, rather than anticipates, social change. Thus
the rapidity of social change over the past few decades has created
today's visible lag between the judiciary performance and the
public's need.

> New rights, like those of social security, have been brought
> into being, and older rights of contract and property made
> subject to government regulation and legal control. New social
> interests are pressing for recognition in the courts. Groups
> long inarticulate have found legal spokesmen and are asserting
> grievances long unheard. Each of these developments has
> brought its additional grist to the mills of justice.[5]

A radically changing society with its constantly changing statutes is a challenge to the best legal minds. The changing moral
and ethical codes that tend further to divide an already divisive
society threaten the social cohesiveness for which, at least indi-
rectly, the courts are responsible. To bring justice out of what
may be a morass of legal entanglements or to bring order out
of social chaos is no small task. "With liberty and justice for all"
can seem an impossible charge.

Chief Justice Burger has noted the tremendous impact these
changes have had on the courts:

> . . . Entirely new kinds of cases have been added because
> of economic and social changes, new laws passed by Congress
> and decisions of the courts. All this represents the inevitability
> of change and progress.
>
> In this 20th Century, wars, social upheaval, and the inven-
> tiveness of Man have altered individual lives and society.

The automobile, for example, did more than change the courting habits of American youth—it paved the continent with concrete and black top; it created the most mobile society on earth with all its dislocations; it led people from rural areas to crowd the unprepared cities. The same automobile that altered our society also maimed and killed more persons than all our wars combined and brought into the courts thousands of injury and death cases which did not exist in 1900. Today automobile cases are the largest single category of civil cases in the courts.

All this ferment of wars, mobility of people, congestion in the cities, and social changes produced dislocations and unrest that contributed to an enormous increase in the rate of crime. In a free society such as ours these social and economic upheavals tend to wind up on the doorsteps of the courts. Some of this is because of new laws and decisions and some because of a tendency that is unique to America to look to the courts to solve all problems.[6]

The mobility of individuals and the resultant congestion have produced a focusing, rather than a leveling, effect on the distribution of case loads. As individuals and groups press for new rights or for protection in the exercise of old rights, other individuals and groups take an opposite position. They cannot see that the granting of new rights to other individuals or groups in no way denies them any of the rights that are inherently theirs. Nonetheless the courts have to deal with the problems that individuals in their lack of logic and rationality fail to handle outside the court setting.

The courts are burdened with litigation based upon technicalities utilized to circumvent decisions already handed down. A prime example is that of the number of cases and the number of years of litigation spent on suits involving school desegregation. The children suffer while adults try to negate decisions designed to guarantee equal educational opportunity to all Americans. The doctrine that separate cannot be equal is ignored in an emotional climate sparked by racism and political maneuvering. It seems that as each case is decided a new technicality places that case or other cases on some court docket.

School desegregation cases represent one facet of social change that has resulted in increasing case loads. Equal employment opportunity, fair housing, environmental problems, and the growth of and concern with "new property" produce additional cases for the courts. Charles Reich, in discussing one of the crucial aspects of today's society, says:

But today more and more of our wealth takes the form of rights or status rather than of tangible goods. An individual's profession or occupation is a prime example. To many others, a job with a particular employer is the principal form of wealth. A profession or a job is frequently more valuable than a house or a bank account, for a new house can be bought, and a new bank account created, once a profession or job is secure. For the jobless, their status as governmentally assisted or insured persons may be the main source of subsistence.[7]

. . .

To the individual, these new forms, such as a profession, job, or right to receive income, are the basis of his various statuses in society, and may therefore be the most meaningful and distinctive wealth he possesses.[8]

More and more, the courts are becoming the vehicle used by the individual to protect his new status or his new wealth.

The individual and his problems are not the only causes of increased case loads. The growing dependency upon the governmental largess and the meaning of this growth and power can translate itself into litigation.

When government—national, state, or local—hands out something of value, whether a relief check or a television license, government's power grows forthwith; it automatically gains such power as is necessary and proper to supervise its largess. It obtains new rights to investigate, to regulate, and to punish.[9]

Subsequently, the potential for resultant litigation of disputes involving governmental largess is also increased. Where a governmental contract replaces a handshake, an expensive court process can replace friendly compromise.

Case load should not be discussed as a universal. As in any situation there are variances. For example, state and local courts handle approximately three million cases annually while the federal courts handle roughly 140,000: "About 90 percent of these cases are disposed of in the lower courts—primarily those in urban jurisdictions—where the dockets are heaviest and the most severe problems lie."[10]

It must be pointed out also that the size of the city has some effect upon the size of the court docket:

In the federal courts today the problem areas are essentially
in large cities. Here we find in the judicial system no more
than a reflection of the complexities created by population
growth and the shift to large urban centers. The problems
exist where the action is.

In Maine, for example, there is only one federal District
Judge and literally not enough for him to do. As a result
he has, for 15 years or more, accepted assignments to go
to courts all over the country where help was desperately
needed. Many judges in the less busy districts have done
the same. It is in the large centers that both civil and criminal
cases are unreasonably delayed and it is there that the weaknesses of our judicial machinery show up.[11]

Another complicating factor is the changing mechanics of
the trial process itself, as indicated by Chief Justice Burger:

Experienced district judges note that the actual trial of a
criminal case now takes twice as long as it did 10 years ago
because of the closer scrutiny we now demand as to such
things as confessions, identification of witnesses, and evidence
seized by the police, before depriving any person of his freedom. These changes represent a deliberate commitment on
our part—some by judicial decision and some by legislation—
to values higher than pure efficiency when we are dealing
with human liberty. The impact of all the new factors—and
they are many and complex—has been felt in both state and
federal courts.[12]

A problem not overlooked, but one for which no satisfactory
general solution has been found, is that involving persons awaiting
trial. Some individuals spend "hard time" in jail while awaiting
trial. This embitters them and exposes society to a new, cynical,
and distrustful person—who otherwise might have paid his or her
due to society and emerged a productive and outstanding citizen.
On the other hand, the crowded docket may become a haven for
a legally wise felon who escapes incarceration and spends his time
committing other crimes until his case is called. The public is out-
raged and frightened when it hears that a crime especially a violent
offense, has been committed by someone who is out on bail. Yet
it ignores the incarcerated individual with an excessive sentence
or it abdicates its responsibility to provide the support necessary
to correct these ills.

The pressing need for more courts is not new; nor is the dire need for expanded and improved jail facilities. Judges, lawyers, and ordinary citizens have decried this intolerable situation, but apparently we see indicted persons as less than human and therefore not requiring human services or humane conditions of living. As a result, the backlog of cases in some courts continues to hinder the cause of justice.

Our constitutions indicate that a citizen is entitled to a "speedy and fair trial." The innocent who must suffer long delays before having the opportunity to be *proved* innocent have every reason to question public morality when it appears to be so insensitive to the needs of a system that is provided to protect sacred human rights.

Many of us will have occasion to deal with a court. Traffic citations, zoning disputes, questions involving city ordinances, and litigation of financial disagreements can necessitate court appearances. Approximately 35 million Americans, for example, have some dealings with "minor courts" each year, 20 to 30 million of whom are charged with traffic violations.[13] In a democratic society the court systems play an essential role in seeing that neither license nor tyranny becomes dominant. Chief Justice Burger has noted both the necessity and the difficulty of this task:

> A sense of confidence in the courts is essential to maintain the fabric of ordered liberty for a free people and three things could destroy that confidence and do incalculable damage to society:
> That people come to believe that inefficiency and delay will drain even a just judgment of its value;
> That people who have long been exploited in the smaller transactions of daily life come to believe that courts cannot vindicate their legal rights from fraud and over-reaching;
> That people come to believe the Law—in the larger sense— cannot fulfill its primary function to protect them and their families in their homes, at their work, and on the public streets.[14]

An individual who must spend time in jail because he is unable to afford bail or because he may not be released on his own recognizance cannot appreciate the many reasons given for the repeated postponement of his trial. He is in no position to have sympathy for crowded dockets resulting from "social change," "new interpretation of laws," or any of the other reasons given, no matter how plausible. The individual awaiting trial, as well as the significant others in his life, interprets delay as injustice. In a sense he is right.

Crowded court dockets are directly related to spending priorities. No one denies that more courts are needed, but meeting that need is a slow and arduous process. It appears that domestic needs are last on the list of priorities. Our major domestic thrust of "law and order" received almost unlimited funding for armament, surveillance equipment, special riot training, and other hardware and programs designed for suppression. But studies show an embarrasingly small amount of money spent on courts, jail improvements, or programs of prevention and rehabilitation. This is not to say that hardware (but not tanks and weapons outlawed for war use), surveillance equipment, and other sophisticated means of crime prevention and apprehension are not important. It is to say that expenditures for such things in the past should have been carefully examined. A review of grants requested under the Omnibus Crime Bill caused great concern among some LEAA (Law Enforcement Assistance Administration) officials who saw the discrepancy between monies requested for well-rounded crime prevention programs and monies requested for riot equipment. Suppression may remove a symptom, but if the cause of a problem is not eliminated the problem will remain and can get worse.

High priority should be assigned to expenditures for additional courts, improved prison and jail conditions, and adequate training for all individuals who are a part of the criminal justice system. Permitting spending priorities to deny individuals the right to a fair and speedy trial would appear to be criminal in itself.

In the minds of many, *judge* and *court* are synonymous terms. This confusion is understandable because of the position that the judge holds in court and the tremendous responsibility that is his. Appointment or election to the bench is an honor. It suggests that the individual so selected is above reproach, is almost impeccable in his morality, is almost indisputable in his wisdom, and, above all, is impartial and fair. History has indicated that this is not always the case. Finding the *perfect* judge may be an impossible task. However, in view of the power assigned his or her high office, it is mandatory that every effort be made to select the best possible person.

In his study of the courts, Howard James determined that 10,000 of the approximately 15,000 persons presiding over courts are not lawyers.[15]

> If my sampling is a fair indication (I simply sat down in
> courtrooms selected at random around the country and lis-

tened), perhaps half of the trial judges are, for one reason or another, unfit to sit on the bench.

Because so little attention is paid to minor-court judges, and because so many are housewives, gas-station attendants, farmers, retired workers, and businessmen rather than qualified lawyers, incompetence on the lower-court bench is far more widespread than in the trial courts. Probably not more than one in 10 lower-court magistrates is, in most states, really qualified to dispense justice today.[16]

Just as many policemen are woefully undertrained for their sensitive jobs, so, unfortunately, are too many judges.

The most basic requirement for a competent judge is that he know law. Yet 14 States do not require their appellate judges to be learned in the law, all of them do not make this requirement for trial judges either. Half of the States do not stipulate a minimum period of legal training and experience for judges at these levels. And the overwhelming majority of the 33 States with justices-of-the-peace have no formal training requirement for them.[17]

One wonders about the promise both of a fair and impartial hearing and of equal protection under the law when the individuals in whose hands final judgment may rest lack adequate preparation for their responsibility. The decision handed down by a judge can have a lasting effect upon the lives of countless individuals. The office and the person chosen for the office should be of unquestionable integrity and preparation. Josiah Gilbert Holland may have had the judge in mind when he penned his poem:

God Give Us Men! A time like this demands
Strong minds, great hearts, true faith, and ready hands;
Men whom the lust of office does not kill;
Men whom the spoils of office cannot buy;
Men who possess opinions and a will;
Men who have honor; men who will not lie;
Men who can stand before a demagogue
And damn his treacherous flatteries without winking!
Tall men, sun-crowned, who live above the fog
In public duty and in private thinking;
For while the rabble, with their thumb-worn creeds,
Their large professions and their little deeds,
Mingle in selfish strife, Lo! freedom weeps,
Wrong rules the land while awaiting Justice sleeps.[18]

The trial judge is a crucial human variable in federal cases, where he commands almost autocratic control over the selection of a jury.

> He decides which questions are to be asked, by whom, and
> to what depth; he also determines the number of peremptory
> challenges (dismissals without explanation) available to each
> side and the rules for their use. If a Federal judge wills it,
> a jury for an important case can be chosen in several hours,
> as happened in the Dr. Benjamin Spock case.[19]

The trial judge also determines whether or not the jury will be sequestered, a potentially critical decision in view of recent arguments. In some cases, for example, a sequestered juror may come to resent the time his jury service is keeping him from his business or family. If he becomes angry, he may vent his frustration on the defendants, whom he considers responsible for this time-consuming process in the first place. On the other hand, sequestration may be advantageous to the defendant by eliminating potentially prejudicial contact between the juror and his friends or biased news media. Furthermore, the probability of being sequestered can serve to filter out potential jurors who don't take their commitment seriously.

The judge must be one who cannot be swayed by public pressure or personal whim. Fairness should be his goal.

> A local district court judge is subject to the particular pres-
> sures of public image, on one hand, and the crowded docket
> of the higher trial court on the other. Most district court
> judges practice law for many years in the town or city where
> the court is located, and were "elevated" to the bench when
> their party came to power in the State House. The unseen,
> and usually unacknowledged, pressure on them to reflect and
> preserve traditional community values can be easily under-
> stood in terms of their background and governmental ties.
> While they are willing to give lenient treatment to a young
> mother on welfare charged with shoplifting, they show no
> such judicial sympathy for a young college dropout similarly
> charged who is loosely identified with radical politics by the
> local police. Consequently, the "attempted murder" charge
> which after the probable cause hearing turns out to be merely
> a case of simple assault and battery is still sent to the grand
> jury. So, too, is the "car theft" felony against a black eighteen-
> year-old who has no adult record, despite a pre-hearing agree-
> ment between defense counsel and the police to reduce the

charges to a misdemeanor. Both occur because the judge says
he does not want a "whitewash" in his court. But the "breaking
and entering in the nighttime" case, in which the defendant
was caught inside the store with money from the broken cash
register, is disposed of in the district court with a light jail
sentence to avoid crowding the higher court with an appeal.
This was achieved only after defense counsel was asked by
the judge how high a sentence he would accept and not
appeal.[20]

The attitude of the judge is an important variable in the entire
judicial process. The latitude given to him is awesome. Rendering
decision is no trivial matter and must be predicated upon studied
consideration of all facts as well as an in-depth understanding
of the very essence of the law. The ruling of the judge, as earlier
indicated, can have wide-ranging effects. As noted by a presidential
commission, a judge's ruling affects not only the person before
him but also other people within the criminal justice system:

> A judge's attitude toward prosecutions for certain offenses
> also affects arrest practices of the police. In one large city,
> for example, it was noted that the number of arrests for prosti-
> tution and soliciation declined sharply during the months that
> a judge who routinely dismissed such cases was sitting in
> the misdemeanor division.
>   . . . It is not uncommon for individual judges to regard
> certain offenses as too trivial to merit any substantial penalty
> or even to merit the court's time in hearing them. An experi-
> enced prosecutor is reluctant to antagonize the judge by bring-
> ing these cases to court despite the availability of sufficient
> evidence to convict the defendant.[21]

Human fallibility can greatly complicate the already difficult
job of the judge. His constant exposure to political corruption and
situations involving conflict of interest can make his work most
frustrating. Unfortunately, some judges do not have the strength
of character to withstand temptation. To further complicate the
matter, the laws of some states subject a judge to situations which
lead easily to misconduct. "Many judges are deeply embedded
in politics, or owe allegiance to a political boss who may be able
to influence decisions."[22]

Just as a police officer can have his·effectiveness compromised
by incidents of corruption, a judge can have his moral authority
lessened through conflicts of interest. For example, in five of the

33 states where the nonurban lower court is the justice-of-the-peace court, the judge is at least partially compensated by his conviction fees.[23] While part-time judges are surely more susceptible to conflict-of-interest cases, all states having justice-of-the-peace courts allow the judge to have other work, and 14 states, in 1968, allowed other lower court judges to serve on the bench part-time.[24] In addition, a judge, like most of us, may have personal problems which can affect his performance. Alcoholism, for instance, is regarded by many as "one of the most serious problems of the bench."[25] Yet, in a sense the judge is above the law in some states; in others, methods of censuring him are so cumbersome as to be tantamount to placing him above the law. "Twenty-two States have no provisions for disciplining judges of general trial courts other than the cumbersome and largely ineffective methods of impeachment, legislative address or recall."[26]

Close scrutiny of the high office of judge gives one pause when the background of research related to that office is considered. At the same time the stress of the office and the variety of matters handled by it cannot be overlooked. Very often the quality of the judge's decision is affected more by the situation than by any character weakness judge may have.

> The quality of district court justice is also adversely affected by the variety of matters the judges must handle. In Massachusetts, a district court judge can hear, all in the same morning, cases which would be heard by four different judges sitting in separate sessions in other states (i.e., criminal cases, traffic cases, family matters, and juvenile cases). It is virtually impossible for a district court judge who at 9:30 A.M. handles a number of adult cases (including those of eighteen- to twenty-year-olds) to shift his entire judicial outlook and philosophy to properly conduct juvenile court at 10:30 A.M. Considering the caseload and the significance of the juvenile court experience for the individual young person, it is a sad comment that Massachusetts has only three special juvenile courts, and that yearly more than 14 thousand juvenile cases are handled in other courts.[27]

It is most difficult to sit in judgment of another under even the best of circumstances, for personal bias is always a force in human nature. The judge (being human) must overcome any such bias. Too, there are always extraneous factors that present themselves at various levels of conscious activity and must be weighed carefully and objectively when a decision is being rendered. In addition to all other observations, the judge must be alert for legal maneuvers (often more properly called "legal machinations") used by the lawyer in an effort to win his case. A thorough knowledge of the law and the ability to get directly at facts without being deterred are mandatory. Wisdom and virtue are high-sounding concepts that must form the very base upon which judgments are made.

There are many variables that give rise to what at times is a wide discrepancy between the theory of law and the way it works in practice. Human error in judgment is only one of the factors that may account for the occurrence of injustices despite all endeavors to perfect a system for safeguarding human rights. Personality conflicts, bigotry, egocentrism, and at times criminal unprofessionalism can thwart the cause of justice—even in high office. Of course underfinancing always plays a role.

Problems faced by the courts are not new. Nonetheless they bear repeating, if for no other reason than to awaken a sleeping public, arouse an apathetic majority, or educate the ignorant masses. If an ordered society is to exist, individuals must become active and concerned *before* they themselves are caught in the intricacies of the judicial network. Their emotional involvement at that time may render them less capable of objective behavior, thereby diluting any positive contribution to the judicial arena. The courts will function in no more efficient manner than informed citizens demand of them.

As has been indicated, breakdowns can take place in many areas of our criminal justice system. This is only one example, but it is an obvious one and it must be corrected if there is to be justice. Functions of the courts must not be curtailed by inadequate funding, an insufficient number of highly qualified and impartial judges, or a public that is apathetic or unaware. Decisions of life and death are made here. Regardless of the nature or type of court, it is a public arena where real, live drama is presented on the stage of life. On any day, any person may become the featured participant. It is imperative that justice handle the curtain.

CHAPTER 5

REPRESENTATION BY COUNSEL AND JURY EXCLUSION

Representation by counsel is an integral part of our adversary system of justice. The right to counsel is one of the most fundamental of the due process rights guaranteed the individual in a court proceeding.[1] If the courts are essential to justice, adequate representation by counsel is essential to the courts. Structurally, law can be an esoteric maze to the layman and particularly to the poor and to minorities who historically have been denied access to power in America. The historical method of operation of the courts and of police has caused most minority group citizens to trust neither. Their hope and the hope and fate of most individuals must rest with counsel. Lack of counsel or inadequate representation by counsel usually assures guilt at least by default. If citizens are not adequately represented by counsel, they are unlikely to fare well in courtrooms and their negative image of legal processes is thus reinforced.

The nature of courtroom procedure is such that few lawyers would seek to defend themselves should the occasion arise. In fact, from the legal profession comes the statement: A lawyer who seeks to defend himself has a fool for a client. This statement alone should be proof positive of the need for highly trained and highly qualified legal assistance in situations requiring the services of a lawyer. For many citizens representation by counsel is not a simple matter.

One of the major problems, if not *the* major problem, in this element of the criminal justice system is the cost factor and its possible meaning. Too often money has an effect upon judicial outcome. That is, the very rich usually have an unfair advantage over the poor. The fact that they can hire the best legal minds is only one facet of this discriminatory situation. The court may find it impossible not to render judgments on the basis of economic capability that translates itself into excellent (if sometimes questionable) counsel. It is true that many prominent persons are found guilty as charged, but how many minority group or poor persons would be found not guilty as charged if they had had access to the same expertise accorded the rich and powerful?

It appears to be common knowledge that many noted attorneys have achieved acclaim for their successful defense of wealthy individuals. Although found innocent or convicted of lesser crimes, the accused wealthy often owe the verdict to the astute handling of a particular case by a clever attorney. Some lawyers (and more especially defense attorneys for persons of questionable character and/or reputation) are said to exact high fees from their clientele in order to be able to prepare a successful defense, despite rather indisputable evidence pointing to the guilt of the client. Legal maneuvers and the use of technical points of law by experienced counsel have been known to result in acquittals for wealthy clients who otherwise would have received prison terms. Seldom are the poor able to avail themselves of the type of attorney usually readily available to the rich. Americans tend to associate quality with price, and too frequently this quality-expense parallel infects our courtrooms. While this situation is permitted to obtain, justice for the have-nots will be more a matter of chance than of design.

Two methods are being employed to alleviate this weakness in our court system, but neither has served to balance the quality-price aspect of the situation. Both methods provide counsel for the indigent. In one approach, court-paid attorneys are appointed by judges to defend individuals who cannot afford private counsel. This system is used in 2900 of our 3100 counties, but unfortunately these appointed attorneys often lack experience in criminal cases.[2] They do not have the phalanx of resources necessary to prepare an adequate defense: monies to pay for investigating expenses and for calling expert witnesses, and a qualified and adequate staff. Only one-fifth of the states, including the District of Columbia, compensate appointed lawyers for their own expenses.[3] This situation would cause even the most dedicated barrister to lose his zeal if confronted by a flood of indigent defendants.

Trials devour both time and money, and it is understandable that the minuscule fees usually paid court-appointed attorneys might encourage them to plead their clients guilty in order to economize, especially if the sentencing is not likely to be severe.

The important fact here is that the client might be innocent, and, given time and resources, the court-appointed lawyer might possibly have proved him so. Deprived of this careful investigation of his case, the accused may become bitter and ultimately apathetic, passing on his bad experiences to others. The latter then become a part of the distrusting mass who have no reason to believe that they can receive justice in the courts.

The backlog of cases usually facing the courts also contributes to the possibility that an attorney will plead his client guilty. In return for a negotiated sentence, the accused indigent will often spend *less* time behind bars while awaiting his trial (even if innocent) than he would should he contest his case. In America, minority status and indigent status often coincide, and when they do, the problems are compounded. Being both poor and a member of a minority group does not imply a lack of sensitivity to injustice. Rather, the individual is possibly much more sensitive, although he may not openly display his feelings. The bitterness at his treatment takes on a double dimension, and he may either harbor a deep-seated hostility and feeling of impotent rage or seek unhealthy or illegal redress for what he sees as a justified grievance. In the latter case, injustice *can* breed crime and *does* breed crime.

The peculiar lexicon of the legal world, added to cultural-lingual differences between many attorneys and their minority group clients, may further alienate the accused from the legal process determining his future. Little attention is paid to the communication problem that may exist between a lawyer and his client, particularly if both speak English. We become highly agitated about bridging cultural-lingual gaps in schools, in churches, and among various social groups, but there appears to be no thrust to ensure that lawyers can really communicate with their clients, regardless of cultural background. Yet the future of a client usually depends upon the closest of cooperation and best of communication with his counsel. This is surely an area for study.

The office of public defender was established as another means of assuring counsel for those who could not afford it. Though being in no better position than the court-appointed attorney in the area of communication, the public defender may enjoy other advantages. For example, usually he has a more substantial staff, records of succeeding cases, and the like. And he is saved the ethical nicety of choosing whether he will devote his time and resources to an indigent or a paying client. Nonetheless, the staff and monies provided may be inadequate to his work load. Public defenders, like court-appointed attorneys, often are forced to negotiate freedom or imprisonment of their clients because of the case backlog confronting the courts. Thus, despite efforts to guarantee adequate representation by counsel to persons who cannot afford to pay for the services of a lawyer, the indigent are likely to be denied access to the best legal counsel or to those "extras" that would improve their chances for equal protection in the courts.

In addition to other problems related to court-appointed attorneys and public defenders, minorities and the poor frequently find legal advice lacking at crucial times. In 32 states courts assign counsel at arraignment, but only five states provide representation at preliminary hearings where cases can be dismissed.[4] Provision for counsel at sentencing was lacking in 75 of 300 counties surveyed by the ABA (American Bar Association).[5] This is especially serious because a persuasive lawyer can often secure a probated or lessened sentence for his client if he is present at an appropriate time.

Still another problem facing the indigent is his entitlement to legal counsel. In *Gideon* v. *Wainwright* (1963), the United States Supreme Court ruled indigents accused in felony cases are entitled to legal counsel, but this principle has not been applied to misdemeanor or civil cases. An ABA survey found that only 120 of 300 counties provided legal representation in misdemeanor cases.[6] While at least one-half of the 300,000 people annually charged with felonies cannot afford attorneys, most counties provide inadequate counsel for the indigent.[7]

The major alternatives to court-appointed lawyers and public defenders are private lawyers and legal aid organizations. Private lawyers can ill afford to give much of their time to clients who cannot pay for services. Nevertheless, there are lawyers who devote part of their time to helping the poor. Particularly is this a growing trend among black and Mexican-American lawyers, many of whom are joining socially conscious, active white lawyers in this endeavor.

Fifty-two percent of rural Spanish-surname families of the Southwest and 31 percent of Spanish-surname families in urban areas had incomes under $3000 in 1959.[8] Although the income figure may have changed, the level of poverty seems to remain about the same, in view of an increasing economic crisis. Moreover, roughly 2 percent of the lawyers in the Southwest are Mexican-Americans, whereas Mexican-Americans compose about 12 percent of the area's total population.[9] It is not mandatory that Mexican-Americans be defended by Mexican-American attorneys, but a language barrier would certainly be more likely to exist for the economically and socially deprived Mexican-American than for the more affluent members of this minority group. Hence the real need for legal services from Mexican-American lawyers who presumably understand both the language and any cultural aspects of the situation better than an attorney from another cultural group—unless that attorney has special experience in the area. Of course, not *all* Mexican-American lawyers can better serve a Mexican-American clientele. On the whole, however, in specific situations of this nature, the communications problem is probably lessened if the lawyer speaks Spanish and is community oriented.

In many respects, the situation among blacks is similar. It raises the question concerning the need for more minority group lawyers—if only to bridge the cultural gaps and help the courts understand behaviors resulting from experiences not understood by white America. How many judges *really understand* the "black experience" or the "brown experience" in America? How many lawyers can speak for these experiences when presenting a case, particularly when such experiences may be the deciding factor in the guilt or innocence of the defendant or the degree of punishment assessed?

One of the more encouraging developments of recent years is the work of legal aid organizations. Unfortunately, groups receiving OEO funds cannot handle criminal cases; even so, the work load is awesome. Also, they cannot solicit clients, being required to retain a professional stance of client-attorney relationship. Thus, many citizens may not know of potential help, while the specter of law and courts may deter others from seeking legal redress. Legal aid groups derive goodly portions of their funding from the government, and the program's sometimes controversial work has made it a political target.

Consequently, it is not surprising that again, in a critical area of administering justice, the response is inadequate to the need.

> The National Legal Aid and Defenders Association indicated there were 900 defenders in the United States in 1966 and half of them didn't work full time. But the need for defenders of the indigent is placed at 8,300 to 12,500 full-time attorneys.[10]

Two private groups, the Fund for the Defense (a predominately black organization) and the Mexican-American Legal Defense Fund, are proving to be a kind of salvation for minority groups and the poor, regardless of race or ethnicity. Here, the right to counsel is not abridged by cost, quality of counsel, or cultural chasm. However, the pressing need for more minority group lawyers becomes apparent. The effectiveness of both the

Mexican-American Legal Defense Fund and the Fund for the Defense can be increased by the active participation of highly qualified Mexican-American and black attorneys. This may become the most viable vehicle for affording quality counsel to minorities and the poor.

It is to be hoped that our system of justice will find a way to safeguard the rights of all Americans without the continuing need to separate by race or socioeconomic status, as if separateness can assure equality.

JURY EXCLUSION

In a democracy a defendant's right to trial by an impartial and representative jury is seen as a fundamental right and as another procedural safeguard against legal abuse. Just as the nature and role of police forces have evolved over the years, so have the nature and role of the courts.

Originally, actual witnesses to infractions comprised the juries. Later juries consisted of a defendant's neighbors. In such cases the eventual verdict was likely to reflect the dominant opinions, interpretations, and biases of the community. Perhaps most importantly, the trial allowed for and encouraged an understanding of the context—economic, emotional, social, and political—of the alleged crime. Perhaps only when these nuances are *felt*, as well as understood, does an accused receive justice, harsh or lenient.

The composition of juries is especially critical at the present time, when defendants are frequently on trial as much for their beliefs as for their acts. The ambiguity and confusion of political cases invite the perhaps undue influence of a juror's political ideology, independent of the facts presented, in arriving at his verdict.

Today, when some people see everything from rape to prayer in schools as a political act, the selection of a jury is regarded as a key factor in the criminal justice process. Indicative of the importance and implications of jury composition is the conspiracy trial of the Harrisburg Seven, accused of planning to, among other things, kidnap Henry Kissinger. Many saw the government's two-million-dollar trial, which ended in a mistrial on the main charges of conspiracy but did find two defendants guilty of smuggling letters, as a blatant attempt by the government to punish these dissidents and intimidate others.

Because of the controversial nature of the trial, a group of social scientists and activists assisted the defense attorneys in selecting a jury. The researchers first did a demographic survey of potential jurors and then interviewed by telephone a proportional sample of registered voters in the judicial district. When the two samples were found statistically dissimilar, the finding was presented to the presiding judge, who, partially on this basis, selected a new panel of potential jurors.

The researchers then conducted more in-depth interviews with a group representative of potential jurors. From this survey the defense sought to derive a correlation between a potential juror's attitudes and his ability to be an impartial juror.

While the defense relied on rumor as well as their own data and avoided behavioral equations, they both affected the trial and raised important questions. As previously noted, they influenced the composition of the juror pool and contributed to the defense attorneys' development of motions and their perception and evaluation of jurors.

But perhaps more significant than the immediate results of the research are the implications for the future. Although the efforts in this particular instance aided the defendants, the possibility of course exists that the government may itself adopt them on a much more sophisticated level.

Furthermore, in gathering the data, the researchers misrepresented themselves, saying they were interested in Harrisburg because of the trial but not saying the information could be used in support of the defendants. The deception was probably essential to securing cooperation, to say nothing of nonbiased findings, but it nonetheless misled the public. While this perhaps seems just a hairsplitting question of ethics, suppose that in future trials both sides misrepresent themselves in a well-intentioned effort to best represent their case? If the experience of recent years is any indication, law enforcement agents can be quite adept at adapting. Within a few years, the trial process might become a competition in sophistication, and ultimately the courtrooms might so effectively predict and control the human variables that the justice dispensed would be no justice at all.

In theory, America is a nation of law where minority rights are protected from majority excesses; where the administration of justice from Watts to the Supreme Court chambers is color blind; where legal niceties, from a policeman's reading a suspect his rights to a trial by one's peers, protect and enhance our liberty.

Yet we have seen stunning lapses of justice, despite the theory and the complex machinery set up to fulfill the philosophy and goals implicit in its underlying principles. The promise of a fair and impartial trial has not always been realized because defendants have not always had the benefit of a fair and impartial jury. Whereas the jury selection process leaves much to be desired, the practice of jury exclusion certainly subverts the ends of justice.

The black in the South has a history of being the most victimized by this discriminatory act. As late as 1965 the Supreme Court in *Swain* v. *Alabama* upheld the conviction of a black defendant accused of rape and convicted by an all-white jury in a county where no black juror had served in 15 years.[11] In that case, as so frequently happens, potential minority jurists were dismissed through peremptory challenges. The use of peremptory challenge is accepted court procedure and is designed to assure proper jury selection by eliminating individuals who may render decisions based not on fact but rather on subjective or prejudicial grounds. However, there is a body of literature that indicates clearly how this very tool, designed to assist the ends of justice, may be used to obstruct it—but legally. And it *was* so used for decades preceding recent court decisions trying to assure more equitable and representative jury selection procedures where minority defendants are concerned.

Just as past and present findings validate the unequal treatment of minorities by law enforcement officers, they reveal in bold perspective the unbelievable discriminatory practices against blacks by the courts, especially in the South. For years, where blacks were accorded the right of a trial, the entire court procedure was a travesty of justice. Traditionally, jurors were all white, and most of them brought their verdicts to the trial. Those opposed dared not voice their opinions for fear of reprisal. "Legal" lynchings were commonplace and served to "warn niggers to stay in their place," particularly when the "crimes" were against whites. Even "disrespect" could result in the death of a Negro. One Negro was hanged for "leering" at a white woman, despite his plea that he really didn't even see the "victim." Reports on the case indicated that the sentence of death was based on the defendant's being "dangerous to the community."

Although many major white-owned newspapers carried stories about the infamous practice of jury exclusion, full accounts of courtroom atmosphere and the disgraceful conduct of juries could be found in the larger black-owned publications. The real flavor of the result of the odious practice was captured by these newspapers, but years were to pass before the federal government would act to halt it. In the meantime, all-white juries continued to dispense southern justice.

All-white juries continued to give quick verdicts of guilty (often not retiring for discussion) for crimes of blacks against whites while dismissing whites for crimes (including murder and rape) against blacks. Similarly little attention was paid to crimes committed by blacks against other blacks. Murder among Negroes was almost rewarded; sentences were suspended or very light. It is reported that the black citizens of Dallas, Texas, at one time had to appeal to the courts for the equal punishment of Negroes for crimes against Negroes. All-white juries were extremely lenient in such cases. No white man has ever been executed for raping a black woman regardless of her age or the extent of the brutality to her body. Reasons given for dismissals or for negligible sentences ranged from "The female [regardless of her youth] admitted or showed evidence of having had sex relations previously" to "The defendant felt that the female, by her actions, enticed him or them to commit the act."

Some of the most incredible verdicts by all-white juries came following the 1954 Supreme Court decision in *Brown* v. *Board of Education* and during the civil rights activities after that historic event. The 1968 Federal Jury Selection Act, endorsing juries representing the spectrum of neighborhood opinion and requiring voter registration lists as a chief jury source, is seen as directly related to malpractices involving jury selection. There are few cases of jury exclusion reported now, but the sharp drop in the practice does not ensure fair and impartial juries. Jury exclusion still exists in fact if biased individuals are selected for jury service in that the defendant still is denied impartial consideration.

Voter registration lists as a jury source are only a partial answer to the problem of jury selection. To rely on registration lists means to ignore many minority citizens, as well as a disaffected segment of the populace no longer participating in electoral politics. Starting with an uneven base produces an unrepresentative result. For example, a New York federal grand jury list was shown to have 1.1 of every 10,000 Harlem voters, but 62.6 of every 10,000 voters from the mainly white (and wealthier) East Side.[12] It is likely that many analogous situations can be found across the country, particularly in smaller urban settings and in rural areas. Whether the selection is for federal grand jury service or service on other types of juries, the principles of selection as they relate to objectivity in decision-making must be the same. The defendant must be accorded the right of just consideration by a jury of his peers.

Our political institutions, no matter how firmly they are locked in a system of checks and balances, are neither inherently democratic nor just. The judicious use, the unintentional misuse, and the willful abuse of political machinery are dependent upon the attitudes of those entrusted with its care. When conviction or callousness supersedes conscience, when ideology replaces morality, or when legality comes to define humanity, even those institutions

originally designed to protect and to promote liberty can become
tools of repression.

In the first part of this book we showed, for example, that
law enforcement agents have frequently ignored the rights and
violated the humanity of individuals, especially those of minority
groups, whether racial or political. This section reveals how the
abuses committed in urine-stenched alleys can carry over into the
courtrooms.

A significant example of the evolutionary nature of institutional safeguards is the grand jury. In theory, a grand jury is to
serve as a watchdog of prosecutors—to monitor their zeal and
to prevent their personal fanaticism from assuming the dimensions
of public policy. Members of a grand jury can play an important
role by conscientiously considering the evidence, or lack of evidence, a prosecuting attorney has, and then accordingly authorizing
or refusing to allow the prosecutor to press charges. The Fifth
Amendment to the Constitution stipulates that an indictment by
a grand jury is necessary in capital cases.

To enable the grand jury to discharge this task effectively,
it was given the power to compel witnesses to testify and to punish
those who refused to do so. Like most political institutions, grand
juries serve the philosophy and wishes of the political faction currently in control. In colonial times, the grand jury alternately protected the rights of Loyalists or radicals. Now, as then, grand juries
tend to reflect the politics of their area. In the past, the grand
jury sometimes, though rarely, asserted its independence to the
point of excluding the prosecuting attorney from its deliberations.
Today such assertiveness is almost nonexistent as some grand jurors
have allowed themselves to become the docile pawns of zealous
prosecutors. Rather than acting as a check on overly ambitious
governmental excursions, grand juries now frequently enhance
those excesses.

Persons ordered to appear before it have no right to be told
what crime, if any, is being investigated or whether they
are being questioned as potential defendants or as mere witnesses. There are no rules of evidence restricting the scope
of the prosecutor's inquiry. Unprotected by the presence of
either judge or legal counsel, witnesses face interrogation that
can reach into virtually any corner of their lives. The prosecutor's unfettered discretion to issue subpoenas to anyone, anywhere, whom he wishes to interrogate is easily transformed
into a power to intimidate and harass advocates of disfavored

ideas. Most importantly, those who are subpoenaed can be jailed if they refuse to cooperate.

But, as the questions that are being asked before today's political grand juries indicate, federal prosecutors are using these powers to elicit political intelligence data on the Administration's critics. They are not attempting to persuade these grand juries to authorize indictments, and the citizens who have been subjected to these improper and pernicious interrogations are, almost without exception, accused of no crime.

In my opinion, the inquisitions are intended to punish and inhibit protected expression and political activity and to break down the private and professional relationships of academic liberals and of political activists. This must be a matter of concern for all of us. The power of compel testimony behind the closed doors of grand jury rooms belongs to whatever political faction wins control of our institutions of government. Today the targets are liberals and radicals—tomorrow's victims may be the Daughters of the American Revolution or the Veterans of Foreign Wars.[13]

Grand juries can be a means either of legally suffocating dissent or of guaranteeing expression. The events of the past few years have left many of us weary of protest in even its mildest forms, and, as recent years have also shown, those most likely to be forced to dissent, in order to survive, are the racial and political minorities. Yet grand jurors are frequently white, middle-class citizens who believe that their way of life is under attack and who accordingly welcome the opportunity to stifle unrest.

The grand jury earned its popular title, "the people's panel," when it served as an instrument of popular government and as the citizen's counterforce to the otherwise unlimited discretion of prosecutors and other officers of government. It was thought to be a crucial link in our system of checks and balances. In the hands of the Nixon Administration its powers have been loaned out to the FBI. The FBI has no authority to force citizens to disclose the details of their personal lives, their political beliefs or associations, their sources of information, their travels, or their conversations with others. The FBI which got almost anything J. Edgar Hoover asked of Congress, was denied the subpoena power he requested to assist his men in gathering just such information. Now this important safeguard has been circumvented. By coupling the unique powers of the people's panel with the FBI's continuing surveillance of political dissenters, an institution designed to protect us from the dangers of a police state has been used to bring us still closer to one.

Little effort is made any more to disguise the extent to which the grand jury's function has been distorted. A Brooklyn grand jury recently was investigating an attempt to break into an FBI office in Long Island. Witnesses reported that while the jurors read magazines and newspapers, the Justice Department prosecutor regularly excused himself to confer with agents of the FBI. Over and over again he returned to ask the same questions that the FBI had been asking the same individuals in its own investigation. It is becoming increasingly clear that the FBI has simply donned the august mantle of our people's panel and seized its powers. This distresses me both because the FBI has concurrently assumed the nature of a political police and because these changes obviously have the approval of the highest Justice Department officers responsible for the conduct of the grand jury proceedings.

The same subpoena power that is being used to satisfy the FBI's curiosity is being used to harass and punish the politically unpopular. It is very intimidating to be hauled before a grand jury, denied a lawyer, and asked: "Who was at this meeting?" or "What was said?" or "Give me the names of everyone you spoke to in March." On the West Coast a grand jury showered more than one hundred subpoenas on individuals engaged in antiwar activities there. No indictments *ever* issued from the proceedings.[14]

Today the grand jury can be still another means of intimidation and harassment of minority citizens.

Proportional representation on juries was seen as one method of protecting minority group defendants from unfair jury decision. Just as proportional representation per se is not the answer to improving police-community relations or police conduct, neither is it a panacea for improper jury composition. Proportional representation and quotas would limit the use of peremptory challenges (which need not in themselves be harmful to a defendant) and could assume farcical dimensions. Moreover, providing mere proportional representation itself does not guarantee the quality of that representation.

Minority group jurors are human and are as vulnerable to need-press as are any other individuals. An upwardly mobile black or Mexican-American seeking acceptance by white America or his fellow jurors may feel that he has to be extra careful not to show leniency to a member of his racial group. Consequently, he may go to extremes in order to show his contempt for crime among his people or to convince his fellow jurors that he is not swayed by racial loyalty. On the other hand, he may be too protective of the defendant in his effort to be "black" or "chicano."

Despite these and other possibilities, minority group representation on juries can be extremely valuable because of the insights that a member of this group may be able to give the white jurors—whether for or against the defendant. It also tends to increase the confidence of blacks and Mexican-Americans that they *may* receive a fair hearing. Finally, it carries out the mandate of the court. Nonetheless, proportional representation and quotas do have limitations, and the defendant is not *guaranteed* impartial consideration simply because a member of his race or ethnic group serves on the jury. On the other hand, the possible disadvantages of an all-white jury must be weighed in particular cases.

Basic objections to all-white juries must be seen in a wider context than that implied in the label "southern justice." The South is not the only section of the country that is guilty of jury exclusion, and blacks are not the only victims of this unjustifiable practice. The historical situation of the Negro in America with its attendant inhuman concomitants simply more sharply defines the insidious aspects of jury exclusion, which is only one more extension of other injustices perpetrated against him. In a sense, presentation of southern justice brings into bold relief the condition of other minorities in all parts of the country.

The black American, despite admitting to fair treatment and even exemplary actions by some all-white juries, has a legitimate concern. The social deprivation forced upon both white and black America as a result of institutionalized racism militates so strongly against fair and impartial judgments by all-white jurors as almost to make a mockery of the endeavor. Despite centuries of living together, sharing a common culture and dying together for the common cause of "freedom," the simple truth is *we don't know each other,* and it seems that all of our institutions are dedicated to maintaining this social isolation. School desegregation is still not a fact because of 20 years of litigation geared to circumventing a unanimous Supreme Court decision declaring that "separate cannot be equal." Although overt violence has abated, hate material against blacks continues to be distributed. The federal government under the Nixon administration included school desegregation in its policy of "benign neglect" of problems of the minorities. The force of white backlash has made clear to black children that they are not wanted in predominately white schools. "Eleven o'clock on Sunday" is still the most segregated hour in America, despite attempts to put the spirit of Christ into Christianity. Families not only move from neighborhoods as blacks move in or as blacks start to attend schools there; some have even left the United States. It is painfully obvious that *no* black—regardless of his political, social, economic, or educational status—is accepted by most Americans as a true equal to a white American. If a person is not *seen* as equal, it is difficult to *judge* him as an equal.

The tremendous political, social, and economic pressures upon the masses of blacks and many Mexican-Americans make upward mobility and endeavors to gain acceptance into the mainstream of society a completely depleting, if not unrewarding, struggle. This reality adds to the already frustrating identity crisis of many minority citizens. These groups, therefore, tend to view the white world with a kind of protective suspicion, if not with hostility. They, in return, may be looked at in the same way—even by persons who *think* they have no such attitudes toward minorities. It is the pervasiveness and insidious nature of bigotry and racism that make it so dangerous. Racism is such an admitted part of the very fabric of our country that few persons escape its psychologically damaging effects.

Many individuals are able to view members of minority groups in America in an objective way. These people are largely responsible for the slow but continuing movement toward true democracy and a mentally healthy society. However, they are obviously a lesser part of the population, or others who share their opinions do not share their courage. Thus, the average minority group citizen constantly faces discriminatory situations. He may be able to handle job discrimination, discrimination in housing, and the like, but if our system of justice fails him, where does he turn? How can he be sure that those who sit in judgment are not going to have their considerations colored by some stereotype? How can he be made to feel secure in the fact that, though all white, the jurors deciding his fate have withstood the impact of racism and will follow the path of other all-white juries in rendering a just verdict? How likely are white jurors to understand the black experience in America or the brown experience in America?

There is no way to guarantee perfect jury selection. It would be impossible to control all of the variables necessary to the accomplishment of this ideal. But if individuals ultimately responsible for proper jury selection will pursue their task diligently and if the American public will take an active interest in the cause of justice, a solution to the problem can be found quickly. In a country where personal value is often equated with earning capacity, it is still possible to prevent miscarriages of justice based on ethnicity or economic status. The following need not happen: A Mexican-American eschewed a $20,000 out-of-court settlement, feeling that he would receive fairer treatment at the hands of a jury. His recompense for faith in the jury system was an award of only $3500 as settlement for an accident which crippled him for life.[15] Strengthening the jury selection process to assure objectivity and fairness to minorities and the indigent will result in objectivity and fairness for all Americans who find themselves defendants in courts of law.

CHAPTER 6

DISCRIMINATORY JAIL SENTENCES AND BAIL BOND PROCEDURES

The Negro, or black, in America is more likely to be the victim of discriminatory jail sentences than is any other racial or ethnic group.

> Once caught, black suspects are more likely than whites to be jailed rather than bailed, more likely to be convicted than acquitted, and more likely to receive stiff sentences.[1]

This is a fact of life for blacks. As a result of continuing experiences with our criminal justice system, they generally expect greater punishment than whites—even for the same crimes. America admittedly has no uniform standard of justice for all and concedes that there is a distinctly different set of rules for its black citizens.

> Southern officials freely admitted to me that there are four standards of justice. First, where white is against white (apart from the absence of sufficient aid to the poor), there is equal protection of the law. Second, where Negro is against Negro, the common complaint is that Southern courts and police are too lenient. One senior official explained to me that Negroes are primitive and emotional, like children or animals, with little sense of right or wrong. If a Negro commits a crime against another Negro he will usually receive a far lighter punishment than a white against white. If anything

the law therefore encourages lawlessness in Negro communities. Third, where a white commits a crime against a Negro, he will be punished lightly if at all, and the Negro complainant may expect reprisals. Rape is a capital offense in all Southern States, but no white has ever been executed for raping a Negro woman. The last time a white was executed in Mississippi for a crime against a Negro was in 1890. Fourth, where a Negro commits a crime against a white, especially an offense against the person, retribution is swift and severe. The statistics on capital punishment are revealing. In Louisiana, between 1900 and 1950, no Louisiana-born white man, and only 2 out-of-state whites, were ever executed for rape, while 41 Negroes were executed for raping white women. No one, Negro or white, was executed for rape of a Negro woman. Since 1956, one white has been executed (for murder), and 10 Negroes (3 for rape). In Mississippi, since 1955, 24 Negroes have been executed, 14 for murder, 9 for rape, and one for armed robbery. In the same period 7 whites were executed, but only one was a Mississippian.[2]

This discriminatory behavior accounts largely for the disproportionate number of blacks in penal institutions. Muhammad Ahmad (s.n. Max Stanford), in his article "We Are All Prisoners of War," estimates that "90% of the prison population in America is black."[3] The stunning truth is that an overwhelming number of blacks are imprisoned in proportion to their representation in the overall population of the country. This situation bears scrutiny and objective study, as do the lesser-publicized conditions that may have sparked our most serious prison disturbances. At the same time that we give special attention to the plight of the black American as regards discriminatory sentencing, instances of this practice that transcend race or ethnicity should be examined.

From interrogation to incarceration, the administration of justice is a reflection of societal values. Our jails and prisons can tell us as much about ourselves as can our schools and libraries. Yet, until a Soledad or an Attica explodes, we cultivate ignorance of penology in order to eschew action on the grounds of lack of knowledge. We sit in our comfortable homes or at the neighborhood bar and condemn all inmates of jails and prisons without hearing their side of the story or without having available to us the kind of unimpeachable evidence prerequisite to judging individuals whose history and way of being are not known to us. The fact that many of our judgments are made upon the basis of stereotype and emotion does not seem to disturb us. That the lives of a large segment of society are adversely and unjustly affected by this attitude seems to have little impact upon our behavior.

Kerper states, "No aspect of the criminal justice process is more crucial to the defendant than sentencing."[4] If the defendant is black and if his sentencing is disproportionate to his offense, the ultimate result may range from sickening surprise to a completely shattered life. Somewhere between these two extremes are found the bitterness, hate, hurt, resentment, impotent rage, and the like, that can spark an Attica or cause destructive prison riots across the country.

As Kerper has pointed out, differences in sentences are common and do not mean *disparity* in sentencing. In fact, differences in sentencing, even for the same crime, are a means of individualizing justice in order to ensure equity. On the other hand, she makes clear the truth that "arbitrary and capricious grounds are unjust and are unacceptable in a democratic society."[5] Judges and jurors in the Old South made no effort to assure impartiality in sentencing. Despite moves to improve sentencing procedures and the development of *Standards* by a committee of the American Bar Association, the many variables related to the history of discriminatory sentencing of blacks will undoubtedly slow reform if not prevent it.

An upsurge of disparate sentencing occurred during the civil rights and antiwar demonstrations. The overreaction of federal, state, and local law enforcement agencies to civil rights and antiwar demonstrators greatly facilitated and encouraged the practice. During the civil rights disturbances, local, state, and federal bodies moved swiftly (and sometimes illegally) to pass harsh laws, often making felonies of acts that were earlier considered misdemeanors. Charges of loitering, threats to the peace, and inciting to riot were lodged against activists for any conduct that could be construed to fall into these categories—or others that carried repressive penalties.

For instance, in some places more than three blacks could not congregate without being charged with loitering. Angry remarks against constituted authority or white racism could make one liable to arrest and sentencing for "threatening the peace." Those who sought to speak to groups (including church groups) about oppressive conditions were vulnerable to a charge of inciting to riot. Maximum penalties were quickly imposed for any type of offense committed by known and admitted black activists. Lee Otis Johnson, a well-known civil rights advocate in Houston, Texas, was sentenced to 30 years in prison for the possession of marijuana. His case received national attention, but the mood of white America appeared to dictate a negative response to appeals, though privately even police officers decried the sentence. In addition, there was, and is, a strong feeling that Mr. Johnson was the victim of a plot to "put him away for good."

The kinds of sentences often imposed upon juveniles resulted in their having records that today make it difficult for many of them to get jobs. In fact, some who want to become police officers or who seek federal or state employment face extreme difficulty in obtaining such positions, despite their qualifications and the dire need for their services. Strenuous efforts are being made to have arrest records stemming from some types of civil rights activities deleted. In the meantime, arrest records can be used by bigots as a legitimate way to deny employment to blacks.

It is discriminatory sentencing, too, when individuals are *not* punished for crimes or when the punishment for a major offense is tantamount to a "slap on the wrist." In the few trials following 186 "serious incidents of racial violence" in Mississippi during the summer of 1964, defendants won acquittals, suspended sentences, or minimal fines.[6] These crimes included mutilation and/or murder of black men, women, and children. Crowds in some of the courtrooms cheered wildly as white defendants were acquitted, received suspended sentences, or were given minimum sentences for their violence against blacks.

The question was often raised: "Had five innocent white children been killed in the bombing of a white church by blacks, what would have been the response?" Among other questions of this nature was: "Had three right-wing activists been brutally murdered, what would have happened to the black activists who killed them?" It might be interesting also to reflect on the kind of response or the kind of sentences that would have resulted had blacks overturned and burned buses, intimidated white children, and threatened law enforcement officers who attempted to protect the innocent children. If past or present history holds the answer, it is obvious that maximum penalties would have been sought and won in each case. This is a damaging commentary on our criteria for sentencing.

The poor and the nonwhite are not the only groups that have been the recipients of discriminatory sentencing. The Vietnam War and the many and varied reactions to it further divided our country. Those who opposed the war became known as dissenters and were seen in a very unfavorable light. They were accused mainly of being disloyal to the president of the United States and of being unpatriotic. Dissenters who were activists (not extremists) began to suffer much the same treatment from law enforcement agencies that blacks had suffered earlier. They were not ruthlessly slain or brutalized to the same degree as were blacks, but some were killed and many were brutalized. All were subject to discriminatory sentencing, and the leaders of some of the movements, and their followers, did receive unfair sentences.

Law is a means of defining a culture. It is only logical that a person from a minority group—whether his minority status derives from his skin color or his political beliefs—may eventually find himself in opposition (perhaps violent opposition) to the individuals and institutions interpreting and enforcing the law. Society essentially represents the imposition (no matter how subtle) of a set of values; a consensual view of "reality"; a methodology of conducting relationships. When we understand and accept this, perchance we will understand the sentencing of Lee Otis Johnson, the gagging of Bobby Seale, the murder of striking farm workers. In addition, we may begin to see our role in an Attica. Dr. Nathan Hare, publisher of *The Black Scholar,* gave permission for the reprinting, in its entirety, of the following article by an individual who had to remain anonymous.

At the time of this writing, the grand jury of Warsaw County, New York, is hearing testimony, and it is expected that numerous indictments will be handed down. The majority of these will be against the prisoners who are considered, in one form or another, participants in the Attica Rebellion. It is also expected that criminal charges will be leveled against certain New York State Troopers, and members of the correction officer staff at Attica Prison. Therefore, prudence, as well as legal considerations, either prohibit or compel the restriction of what is said in print. One must recall the old plantation slave who said, "Everything I tells you am the truth, but they's plenty I can't tell you."

The final and calculated response to the rebellion at Attica Prison, represented the ultimate manifestation of prejudice—extermination! The events of September 9–13, 1971, held the center of the world stage for a few fleeting moments of time and, a year later, that scene has slowly dissolved from the minds of most black people. How easily we forget! Birmingham, Watts, Detroit, Newark, Jackson State, Fred Hampton, George Jackson, and now Attica Prison.

Historically, blacks in America, have been the most apathetic group known to mankind. Even today, as supposedly enlightened people, we bicker and argue, can't decide who shall lead, refuse to marshall our strengths and join together in common cause to achieve basic goals.

As a result of this inability to act collectively, we are like
eunuchs in the harem. We walk around, enjoy the titillating
sights, but our impotence makes it impossible for us to fully
participate. Our political impotence is a damning indictment
in light of our political strengths; and our economic power
is fruitlessly dissipated instead of concentrated in our own
self-interest. Yet, after 400 years, we dare to tell ourselves,
"We are making progress!"

It is this lack of political power and economic strength,
plus the general apathy on the part of black people, that
has allowed the forces supporting institutionalized racism to
flourish uninhibited. Have no doubt that such considerations
were pondered fully before the forces of destruction were
unleashed at Attica. Power has no need to concede anything
to those who are politically impotent.

The prison powerhouse siren gave repeated blasts. That
is a warning to members of the surrounding community to
reach for their righteousness and rifles. A prisoner has es-
caped! Bounty time! This time it was different. A full scale
riot was in progress.

Football-helmeted prisoners, faces made unrecognizable by
masks, had seized control of the prison. Their hostilities and
anger, long suppressed, or rationalized and turned inward
towards each other, exploded and vented in a fury of destruction. Windows were smashed. Furniture destroyed. Doors
broken. Fires set. The atmosphere of violence was contagious,
sweeping all before it, and sometimes leaping ahead like a
fire that has crowned.

The "hacks" (correction officers) who had brutalized the
prisoners through the years, physically and verbally, were
set upon, and their vaunted "nigger sticks" (the clubs they
carried) were torn from their hands. Then it was the prisoners'
turn to inflict upon the "hacks" the degradation and humiliation they were forced to undergo each time they went to
receive a visit from loving members of their families. Each
"hack" captured was forced to remove all his clothing, given
an anal inspection, and then they were taken, naked and
herded into the prison yard. Spontaneously, the Attica Rebellion had begun!

Only a few hours had passed before the huge steel gate
at the rear of the prison slowly rolled open. The brilliant
red fire-engine menacingly eased through. Its windshield was
completely taped, leaving only a slit for the driver to peer
through. The gray-garbed army of occupation briskly filed

through behind the tank-like shield, looking like combat-troops moving into a Vietnamese village in full battle gear. The troopers wore helmets with tightened chin-straps, pistols loose in their holsters, rifles ready at port-arms, three-foot clubs swung on their belts as well as gas masks, and they carried gas guns, including grenade launchers. The fire-engine made numerous trips to the rear gate of the prison, each time escorting in hundreds of troopers who immediately set up outside perimeters. This was all-out war! They came prepared!

The graffiti was scrawled in an area occupied by the troopers at the outset of the rebellion, and patrolled by them throughout the siege. The filthy outpouring is indicative of the authoritarian, pathological and sex-obsessed white mind:

- Black Blood Will Flow Freely. You Bet Your Black Ass
  - Angela Davis Sucks Troopers Dicks
  - The Black Panthers Are Pussys
  - Die, Jackson, Die
  - All Blacks Are Niggers
  - Big Black Mother You LDSE Back to Slavery (Note: the meaning of LDSE is unknown to this writer)

It was an old movie. The villagers had shot a German soldier, and the men of the town had been lined up before a wall for execution. The German commander warned that they could be saved only if the guilty party surrendered. The movie scene held me in total sway and suspense. Then the captain gave the order to fire! It seemed so real—as if it actually happened!

At Attica, when the prisoners defied death, marching the "hacks" and civilians to the top of the tunnel, turning their faces toward the menacing guns of the troopers, a deathly silence swept over the prison. The hostages were stationed yards apart. Some cried. One fainted. Everyone was breathless! Would the troopers shoot them? The captors and captured stood silently waiting. Someone screamed, "Go ahead and shoot, you pig bastards!" The rising sun cast lengthening shadows; the life-span of all the men on the top of that tunnel grew increasingly short. What would be the outcome? Would they live or die? It seemed so unreal—as if it was not happening!!!

We really didn't believe they'd come in with guns and grenades. We expected hand-to-hand combat, and perhaps

gas. When the decoy helicopter started flying its slow, con-
centric circles over the prison yard, narrowing the field until
it was flying tilted, almost directly overhead, we thought they
were taking pictures. Standing on the tunnel we unfurled
our Black Liberation flag, which was colored black, red and
green. As it fluttered back and forth in the breeze, everybody
joyously shouted and waved up to the helicopter. We thought
we were on camera. The world would witness our struggle
for justice. Shortly afterwards, as Harriet Tubman said about
Fort Wagner, "We saw the lightning, and that was the
guns . . . then we heard the rain falling, and that was the
drops of blood falling . . . it was dead men that we reaped."

Yes, I'm a combat veteran. I've seen death and destruction,
and my heart-beat has quickened when the enemy softened
up our area with artillery, mortars, and small arms fire, prior
to an attack. I've heard the thunderous din of an infantry
company, simultaneously discharging their weapons on the
firing range; engaged the enemy in fast-moving combat patrol
and fire-fight actions behind their lines. I've exchanged rapid-
fire from a fixed position as the foe charged.

However, in all my military experiences I've never heard
such deafening, sustained and concentrated gunfire as that
which the troopers and "correction" officers poured into the
defenseless men huddled in the D-Block yard. What a fantas-
tic assortment of man-killing weaponry! Hand guns that
shatter a man's shoulder; rifles that destroy an engine block;
Thompson machine guns whose 45 caliber bullets cut a person's body in half; gas guns and deathly grenade launchers
that maim, decapitate and kill; and shotguns whose pellets
are each capable of inflicting instant death. The real miracle
was that so many men survived. Even now we still do not
know the number of men who were seriously injured and
crippled for life. How many men were driven insane by the
carnage and subsequent brutality? Perhaps we will never find
out!

Gas shrouded the D-Block yard like a deathly mask, and
I tried to escape the oppressive cloud by hugging the ground
and thrusting my face into the mud. Suddenly, an excruciating
kick in my ribs added pain to the nausea I suffered. Paralyzed
with fear, I glanced from the corner of my eye at the towering
apparition above me, masked like some Martian creature.
With a rifle pointed ominously at my head, the creature roared
like a maniac, "Get on your feet you dirty, black nigger bastard! I'll kill all you niggers! Get up nigger!" Still cringing,

I remembered to wipe the mud from my face, then I promptly stood up. In the excitement I placed my hands high in the air. He quivered with rage, eyes dull and vacant, limbs catatonic, shouting, "On your head, nigger! Put 'em on your head, you dirty nigger bastard! I'll kill all you niggers! I'll kill all you niggers!"[7]

The article may need no response, but it should raise some questions. How many men in the prison were victims of disparate sentencing? In view of the graffiti of the troopers and the invectives of the prison guards, how much more self-control and discipline did they exhibit than did the prisoners? How widely representative of the tendency to psychological and emotional disintegration under pressure were the behaviors of the troopers and the guards? Did the graffiti and the invectives represent the basic attitudes of the troopers and the guards? If so, what kinds of both overt and subtle "nasty" behaviors might one expect from guards under *normal* conditions? In what ways do *any* individuals react to racial slurs, threats, or other oppressive behaviors? Finally, if one is being unduly punished already, how might he be expected to react to additional, unnecessary abuse over time?

Disparity in sentencing cannot be accepted in a society that promises equal treatment under the law. The awakening youth of our land have been the victims of injustices and unfair treatment. It is to be hoped and expected that they will not continue to tolerate a hypocritical judicial system. A true and effective democracy can never be achieved in a society rife with chicanery or with justice by whim or unscrupulous political power.

All Americans must continue to remember that each weakness in our criminal justice process affects everyone. Discriminatory sentencing permitted to continue for any segment of society guarantees the vulnerability of all other segments to the same type of treatment. Like a forest fire, "Only you can prevent it!"

BAIL BOND PROCEDURES

In a democracy, one of the cornerstones of the administration of justice is the constitutionally protected presumption of the innocence of the defendant until his guilt is proved beyond doubt. The bail system seeks to accomplish two tasks critical to rendering certain this important civil status. First, it recognizes the right of the defendant to remain out of jail until proved guilty. He can thus continue his normal activities and have an opportunity to help in the building of his defense. Second, a bail system takes into consideration the obligation of the defendant to appear for

trial at an appointed time and seeks to assure the fulfillment of
that responsibility. The functions of a bail bond system, then, are
(1) to balance the defendant's rights with his obligations and (2)
to replace the presumption of guilt associated with jail confinement
with establishment of guilt "beyond reasonable doubt" in the court
of law. The Federal Rules of Criminal Procedure guarantees the
individual's right of bail in noncapital offenses preceding
conviction.[8]

> From the passage of the Judiciary Act of 1789 . . . to the
> present Federal Rules of Criminal Procedure . . . federal law
> has unequivocally provided that a person arrested for a non-
> capital offense shall be admitted to bail. This traditional right
> to freedom before conviction permits the unhampered prepa-
> ration of a defense, and serves to prevent the infliction of
> a punishment prior to conviction. . . . Unless this right to
> bail before trial is preserved, the presumption of innocence,
> secured only after centuries of struggle, would lose its
> meaning.
> The practice of admission to bail, as it has evolved in Anglo-
> American law, is not a device for keeping persons in jail
> upon mere accusation until it is found convenient to give
> them a trial. On the contrary, the spirit of the procedure
> is to enable them to stay out of jail until a trial has found
> them guilty. . . . Admission to bail always involves a risk
> that the accused will take flight. That is a calculated risk
> which the law takes as a price of our system of justice. We
> know that Congress anticipated that bail would enable some
> escapes, because it provided a procedure for dealing with
> them.[9]

Unfortunately, this traditional safeguard can become just another tool of discrimination. Societal responses to a given situation
are partially a result of the visibility of those involved, creating
special problems for minorities in a culture dominated by white
values. Frequently a professional criminal can more easily make
bail than can a minority person because the latter arouses a more
emotional response to his being released. Blacks, for example, are
four times more likely than whites to be jailed without due process
of law on account of bail inequities.[10] Excessive bail bond is another effective tool among the many instruments used for discriminatory practice. Yet the Eighth Amendment to the Constitution
of the United States, as well as the constitutions of many individual
states, contains provisions designed to prevent it: "Excessive bail

shall not be required, nor excessive fines imposed, nor cruel and unusual punishments inflicted."

This is another of those unfortunate situations in which measures taken to protect valuable rights of the individual are circumvented, if not deliberately, and often illegally, ignored. For the poor, this chink in the armor of the bail system increases the likelihood of conviction and imprisonment. Because of their inability to raise bail, 40 percent to 80 percent of large-city defendants are jailed one to eight months *before* trial.[11]

> A bond may cost about 10 percent of the face value of the bond. This money, of course, must be paid whether the accused appears or not. If an accused is forced to use a professional bondsman is he not faced with punishment before guilt is established? He must either pay the bond or must stay in jail until the time of trial. A first offender may have to pay a bondsman more than a well-established crook. . . . Detention prior to trial was found to be quite extended in many cases. In over 45 percent of the non-bail cases, the prisoner was detained over 100 days. . . . About half of all felony defendants are deprived of their freedom before trial and verdict.[12]

In addition, the situation lowers, if not eliminates, a defendant's already meager income, thereby increasing his debts and further reducing any hope of his affording private counsel. Obviously, neither can he develop his own case through personal groundwork. Incarceration, and the attendant loss of wages, often disrupts the defendant's home life, creating material and psychological problems for others as well as for himself. When bond is prohibitive and the accused is confined with convicted criminals, his individual dignity is likely to be demeaned and a psychological climate created for presumption of guilt by some jurors. Significantly, defendants jailed prior to trial are more often convicted and less often given probation than defendants making bail.[13] This finding tends to show a direct relationship between bail bond inequity and conviction or denial of probation. Assuming the accuracy of the relationship, excessive bail can be personally devastating to the accused and precludes any possibility of equal access to justice.

Excessive bail was used as a major weapon against known black and brown militant leaders. Its indiscriminate use during the civil disturbances of the 1960s was sanctioned by the general public, which refused to see the injustice of the excessive bail bond procedure. Society seems to accept unlawful acts if they satisfy an immediate societal need or wish. It makes little distinction between disparate actions and differentiating behaviors. The real danger is the setting of a kind of precedent that further harms our already beleaguered system of justice and must ultimately expose not just minorities but *all* citizens to judicial inequities.

The equity of procedural processes is largely determined by the person or persons administering the guidelines. Humans are prone to honest error; consequently, it must be acknowledged that some inequities are due to honest mistakes.

In the Southwest, for example, it is sometimes not made clear to Mexican-American defendants that the *first* appearance at court is *not* a trial. This misunderstanding can result in the Mexican-American's unintentionally missing his trial, so that he forfeits bail and acquires a criminal record. Such occurrences can be combated through some means of assuring that defendants will be served by conscientious and thorough officials committed to ensuring individual rights. This is mandatory for people who have a language difficulty or who lack the educational background to comprehend their situation.

While mistakes account for some bail bond problems, bail inadequacies sometimes are conscious attempts to discriminate against and intimidate citizens. Often higher bail is set for browns and blacks than for whites who allegedly commit comparable violations. Excessive bail can be intentionally used as yet another form of harassment.

> But sometimes an officer is vindictive and wants to see the defendant punished. So the officer deliberately fails to show up in court. (This is especially true when the policeman knows he is short on evidence.) The result is that the defendant must keep coming back to court until his accuser shows up. Such police-caused delays can cost a man money in time off from work. He may even be held in jail if unable to make bail. The taxpayer foots the bill for his "room and board."[14]

A particularly flagrant abuse of the bail system is described in the following disclosure to the United States Commission on Civil Rights:

> . . . During the harvest season local farmers would go to the jails in the towns of Center and Monte Vista, Colorado

on Monday mornings and inquire about the number of Mexi-can-American laborers arrested over the weekend. The farmers would select the best workers and pay their fines for them. Upon their release the men would have to repay the farmer by working for him. According to Trujillo, in Monte Vista the men were told by the police magistrate that if they did not remain on the farm and work off the amount owed to the farmer, they would be returned to jail. In addition, he said, the police magistrate would sometimes give the farmer a "discount." If the fine was set at $40, he would only require the farmer to pay $25. The magistrate, however, would tell the worker that he owed the farmer $40 worth of work. According to Mr. Trujillo, once the worker was released from jail, he usually was at the mercy of the farmer and often was ill-treated while on the farm. The chief of police and a patrolman in Center, and the police magistrate in Monte Vista confirmed the fact that workers are bailed out of jail or have their fines paid by local farmers and are obligated to work off the ensuing debt.[15]

Other abuses of the bail bond system as it relates to the Mexican-American can be found in the Report of the United States Commission on Civil Rights, *Mexican-Americans and the Administration Justice in the Southwest,* March 1970.

In an endeavor to remedy this denial of human rights some alternatives to the cash bail system have been tried. One is the right of release on the defendant's own recognizance. Originally this privilege was reserved for prominent citizens, but gradually it has been extended to persons who are poorer and less well known. Of course there are many inadequacies and weaknesses in any relatively new program, but experimental programs in which defendants are released from jail *if* they meet qualifications involving family and community ties, residency, employment, and the like, are encouraging. For example, only 1 percent of over 7500 defendants released in two years of the Mecklenburg, North Carolina, Pre-Trial Release Program did not appear for trial.[16] A similar program is being tried in Des Moines, Iowa. The following partial report is heartening:

Appearance for Trial
All available evidence from the Des Moines Pre-Trial Un-supervised Release Program and from bail release in Polk County indicate the same appearance rate, almost ninety-eight percent.

Pre-Trial Offenses
Pre-trial supervision subjects and those released on money bail had the same rate of offense allegations (approximately seventeen and one-half percent) during the release period.

Pre-Trial Jail Time
The pre-trial supervision project during 1971 is estimated to have saved 3,343 defendant jail days. Of these 1,231 days would have been served by defendants who were ultimately not found guilty.

Legal Representation
People released under pre-trial supervision were able, more often then those jailed, to provide their own defense attorneys rather than relying upon court-appointed counsel.

Court Outcome
Pre-trial supervision subjects are less often incarcerated subsequent to conviction than those jailed, although sentence lengths for those who are incarcerated do not differ from those of defendants jailed prior to trial.[17]

Although these data report the degree of success achieved by a program instituted in order to offset the blatant discriminatory practice of excessive bail bond and/or other abuses of the bail system, they give some indication of the number of persons who do, or who may, suffer from inequities in this segment of our system of justice. They should point up the urgency for bail bond reform, but unless the American public becomes aware and concerned, progress will be slow. Innocent people will continue to suffer.

To the professional criminal, imprisonment is an accepted occupational risk. He sees his arrest, trial, and incarceration as bad luck, not an inevitability, and views his crime and detention in crude cost-benefit terms. To a minority nonrecidivist, however, imprisonment is frequently another discriminatory experience. If excessive bail is the cause of his pretrial imprisonment and all of its attendant negative experiences, a potentially productive citizen could join the growing ranks of embittered individuals who have lost faith in even the *possibility* of justice in America.

A just bail bond procedure must be available to *all* citizens. Release on one's own recognizance or any other means of assuring certain human rights must be a complement for that system, not a stopgap because of abuses within it.

PART THREE

THE BLUE
MINORITY

INTRODUCTION TO PART THREE

Part One of *The Administration of Injustice* sought to provide an overview of the manner in which law enforcement agencies have operated historically and still operate at the present time. Documented evidence disclosed the neglect and the abuse of minority citizens by law officers—whether the official misconduct took the form of physical brutality, subtle intimidation, or institutional insensitivity as characterized by inadequate complaint procedures.

The inclusion of negative data regarding police relations with minority citizens represents an effort to get at the truth, *not get the police*. In commenting on the Watts riot, the late Senator Robert Kennedy noted the differences in cultural views of the police. Although he was referring to a specific minority at the time, the same statements hold true for other minority groups:

> There is no point in telling Negroes to obey the law, because
> to many Negroes the law is the enemy.[1]
>
> . . .
>
> We have a long way to go before law means the same
> thing to Negroes as it does to us. . . . The law does not
> fully protect their lives, their dignity or encourage their hope
> and trust for the future. . . . The first step is to move beyond
> the thinking that this is "a Negro problem."[2]

Part Two of this book examined the role of the court system,
with emphasis on its constitutional safeguards and procedural
misfirings.

Part Three returns to the police officer himself. In the opening
chapter of this concluding section, attention is given the assumptions and concepts from which an officer derives his legitimacy.
An awareness of the philosophical basis for the institutionalization
of policing duties is mandatory if one is to perceive the essence
of living in a policed society, or of policing that society.

It is difficult, if not impossible, to understand the riots, the
rhetoric, the repression of the past few years without understanding
the inherently political nature of police work. The conduct or misconduct of law enforcement agents becomes more comprehensible
when one realizes that many officers believe they exist essentially
to perpetuate and protect a given political culture.

This section examines a crucial, but consistently overlooked
condition: the police officer as a member of a minority. Volumes
have been written examining and "explaining" the lives of racial
and ethnic minorities in America. A policeman, however, is a member of an institutional minority, the neglect of which can have
Orwellian implications.

> The police represent not only persons of a subgroup in a
> society, but also a symbol of social values, of authority, of
> formal and codified rules of conduct. The police are the guard-
> ians of a system of values that have historical continuity and
> contemporary coherency; they are the executors of middle
> class values reflected in the criminal law and community
> norms of right and wrong conduct. They are the front line
> reconnaisance troops of these values; their functional role
> is to discover, detect, and deter deviance from those values,
> while protecting vulnerable victims from the offensiveness
> of others. In this sense, the community of individuals is pri-
> marily composed of persons who accept, internalize, and

themselves teach and represent in their roles the very values
the police are expected to uphold.[3]

Just as skin color, hair texture, eyes, and other distinguishing
features serve generally to differentiate racial groups, the uniform
is the most obvious differentiating feature for the police officer.
Nothing draws attention like the badge, the gun, and the "blue."
This distinctive uniform and some of the pressures under which
an officer operates cause the writer to view the police officer as
a member of the *blue minority*.

The physical as well as the psychological ramifications of
this status have in recent years placed law enforcement officers
in a situation analogous to that of members of persecuted minority
groups. *All* police are seen as being alike. The uniform has often
made the police obvious targets for both physical and verbal violence. Individuality is not permitted members of the police profession. Few people really admit that, like any other group, law enforcement officers are neither all good nor all bad. Few positive
assessments are made whereas many negative charges are leveled
at this group.

> The policeman is a "Rorschach" in uniform as he patrols his
> beat. His occupational accouterments—shield, nightstick,
> gun, and summons book—clothe him in a mantle of symbolism
> that stimulates fantasy and projection. Children identify with
> him in the perennial game of "cops and robbers." Teen-agers
> in autos stiffen with compulsive rage or anxiety at the sight
> of the patrol car. To people in trouble the police officer is
> a savior. In another metamorphosis the patrolman becomes
> a fierce ogre that mothers conjure up to frighten their dis-
> obedient youngsters. At one moment the policeman is hero,
> the next, monster.[4]

> Having a police badge does not make men alike. The uniform
> does not cause uniformity of ideas, hopes, aspirations, and
> achievement. While there may be more similarities among
> persons in a police organization than in the community at
> large, each officer comes to his profession with his own pecu-
> liar personality, abilities and talents to handle ideas and
> people. If there are sadists in the police force, they must
> be extremely rare, and the idea is more of a myth than a
> reality. But there are some men more aggressive, more prone
> to violence, more hostile, more prejudicial than others. To
> say that these same variations exist in all occupations is not

a sanguine response, however, for the police are in a special
kind of relationship to the community that most other occupational groups do not enjoy (or suffer).[5]

Yet just as we delude ourselves by saying we know what
it means to be poor because we have seen a documentary on poverty, so do we delude ourselves by thinking we know what it
means to be a policeman because we know something about crime.
We may perceive something of the objective world in which a
poor person or a policeman is expected to function, but the subjective reality, which is often the basis for action of that welfare
recipient or law enforcement agent, escapes us.

The second chapter of this final section considers the special
problems of training and then supervising people who, upon taking
an oath, assume a singular position in our society.

Although most of us, psychologically or materially, are in
either a superior or an inferior position relative to our fellow citizens, an enforcement agent possesses the legitimized recourse to
violence. The highly sensitive situations with which an officer must
cope, the visibility of his deportment arising from his own minority
status, the potential for violence inherent in almost any police intervention, and the ramifications, on both individual and collective
levels, of police action all necessitate thorough training and conscientious supervision.

These same factors explain the need for public understanding
and support of the police—the subject of the third chapter in this
section. As a former attorney general, Senator Robert Kennedy
was aware of this:

> We place our lives and our homes in their hands, yet we
> pay them disgracefully low salaries and force them to moon-
> light. We expect them to expose their lives to danger in our
> behalf, yet we leave their families without adequate life in-
> surance protection. We require them to make split second
> judgments on legal, social and moral questions, yet we do
> not provide them with enough up to date education and train-
> ing opportunities.[6]

The character of a given society is partially defined by the
interaction of its policing agents with other people. Failure to participate in the structuring of society can create a vacuum which
can be filled with overt totalitarianism.

The final chapter of this section presents a model for effective
crime prevention. The aim is to present solutions, rather than just

pose problems; to redresss, rather than harp. Most importantly, the chapter is based, not on merely leisured reflection, but on actual field work in a major metropolitan city.

If the reader feels the book began on a negative note, this model offers a rebuttal, optimistic in its inherent assumption that situations created by humans can be changed by humans. It is hoped that the model will mark for the reader, not the end of a book, but the beginning of self-reflection, of institutional examination, of active compassion.

CHAPTER 7

PAWNS OF POLITICS
AND
OF POWER

Today's law enforcement officer is a political animal. The lowest-ranking officer will admit the strong influence that politics wields within the police profession. In earlier years there was some evidence of endeavors to keep law enforcement free of partisan politics. These efforts, though not completely successful, forced any police political activity underground and to some extent reassured the average citizen that his law enforcement agency was free of political influence.

Suddenly everything changed. The avowed policy of "no political involvement" has been swept aside and replaced by open, partisan politics in some police departments. It was widely reported that members of the Houston (Texas) Police Department were permitted to display Wallace stickers on their trucks and other personal vehicles. Further, high-ranking officials in various cities were said to have hosted fund-raising drives or otherwise to have openly participated in political activity. We are not making a value judgment about such behavior. Whether it is right or wrong is a moot question and one which the average voting citizen has ignored in recent years. Of importance is the undebatable truth that police are definitely in politics. One can only speculate on what this means. An examination of how it may have evolved might prove interesting.

First, the nonpolitical stance mentioned earlier has never been a total reality. It has always been more rhetoric than fact, but a relatively placid society paid little attention—choosing to see its officers as not politically involved. Moreover, the "political involvement" was of a different nature. A good example is shown in what was said about the Minneapolis (Minnesota) police:

> But one of the most significant factors, especially in its implications for other cities, was the politicalized tradition of the police department itself. That tradition dates from the days the police were used to help fill the pockets of corrupt politicians, to the 1930's when they were used to break the workingman's strikes, to the 1960's when they aligned themselves with organized labor to build a political power in their own right.[1]

Until the 1960s there was little strongly organized effort on the part of police to become a political power in their own right. Except for illicit activities that resulted in payoffs by various political figures or that served police interests of a rather minor nature, the policeman as an overt politician did not exist. His role was largely that of protecting and preserving the institutions and legal devices created by the political activity of others in their endeavor to make permanent the temporal. The importance of this role and the responsibility of the police officer is not to be minimized: ". . . The police function is a basic component of man's government by man which has determined the character and permanence of every social structure since human beings first sought collective security."[2] In addition to this important function, law enforcement represents the means by which a government assures its perpetuation and legitimacy:

> A government ought to contain in itself every power requisite to the full accomplishment of the objects committed to its care, and to the complete execution of the trusts for which it is responsible, free from every other control but a regard to the public good and to the sense of the people.[3]

Thus the mandate given to police agencies must at the same time empower police authority to carry out its awesome duty. What we have, then, is a body charged with maintaining a kind of status quo and given almost unlimited power to fulfill its obligation. No wonder law enforcement has been a constant target of politicians and powerful vested interest. Given access to police prerogative, individuals and groups could greatly enhance their positions and use this additional source of power for personal gain. None of this is new information. Widely publicized cases of police corruption attest to long-term political influence in some police departments. The fact that police are beginnning to realize and utilize their power for their own collective benefit *is* new. The evolution of police as a political force may owe its beginning to the awakening of a sleeping giant.

The precipitating factor was more obvious. The awakening, which began slowly, became abrupt with the onset of social change during the latter 1950s and the 1960s. The cop who knew and played with the kids on his beat, who was aware of some political domination but took it in stride, is gone. The new officer is more isolated because he rides in a patrol car. He does not know the people in his patrol area. He finds youth largely hostile or indifferent. Organized crime wears a suit of respectability and is difficult to distinguish from legitimate enterprise. Political intervention in law enforcement and the pervasive influence of the wealthy irk the average officer, who feels (and is) victimized by both.

Finally, he must do his job in an era of societal flux and impatience. Our most staid and revered institutions are being attacked; heretofore inviolable moral and social values are being questioned; our whole system of law and justice is in danger of being subverted; and the questionable ethics of our political leadership is creating an apathetic American public out of our most concerned and enlightened citizens. The police officer must act in a period when increasing numbers of laws deal with private acts and victimless crimes, for example, laws concerning sex, drugs, and political expression. It is his responsibility to intervene in situations in which legal authority is not sure of its ground and to act decisively in the most ambiguous circumstances. At the same time he is not permitted the luxury of error—despite the proliferation of often questionable laws designed to impose limits and structure in a restless time.

The nature of police training, along with the fact that the police officer takes his cues from the segment of the populace that makes and sanctions the laws, forces the officer either to distrust change or to attempt to control it. Additionally, he must actively resist what might be considered unorthodox attempts to bring about social change, though the endeavors may be legal. Yet the flood of change is upon us. What was once a relatively simple decision to arrest or not to arrest has become complex, often with conflicting alternatives.

> The decision to arrest, or to intervene in any other way, results from a comparison, different perhaps for each officer, of the net gain and loss to the suspect, the neighborhood, and the officer himself of various courses of action.[4]

Policemen are statutory beings only in theory. In reality they possess, and must possess for their survival, wide discretion. Yet the same dynamics operate in Hough as in Vietnam: The more an officer intervenes in a situation, the fewer his options. And the decision to intervene or not must often be made in seconds in a volatile atmosphere. Any or all of the almost infinite number of physical and/or psychological variables affecting any individual at any given moment may potentiate a violent episode. The unfortunate, if not unfair, part of all this is that in most cases the officer himself is in no way responsible for the conditions causing the problem. The values, norms, codes, and the like, that he must protect are mandates from others, although he may fully agree with them.

The inexcusable situation created for the police officer often comes from the political arena. Police are consistently exploited by competing politicians and organizations. When election time rolls around, liberal and conservative office-seekers alike pursue the "safe streets" vote. Such self-serving appeals can just make the officer's job harder by imposing impractical demands on him. He is constantly liable to some political whim, for despite arguments to the contrary, his life is in the main politically controlled. The average law enforcement officer is more wary of the politician than any other individual—particularly if the political figure is powerful. Salaries, conditions of work, and many other variables depend in some manner upon duly elected or appointed officials. Not a few seem to take pride in flouting the law or "pulling rank" when stopped or ticketed for a violation. Many a highly professional officer is reluctant to confront a political figure, and if he summons the courage to carry out his responsibility, he admits that the case against the offender probably will not be prosecuted. Thus the officer becomes embittered and may be persuaded that it is possible for some individuals to be above the law.

No politician and no political office can afford to be permitted to be above the law.

A serious point in question is the Watergate affair. If an individual is so closely related to an office that he is considered above the law because the office is above the law, the true meaning of democracy is in danger of being subverted. An office cannot be allowed to take away citizen status before the law and endow the individual with unusual, deified status transcending constitutional laws that make *all* citizens accountable to the people through our system of justice. Successful political moves that circumvent the law would seem to contribute much more to the increase in lawlessness in our country (including political activism) than the so-called riots of the 1960s. When individuals who ride to victory on a law-and-order platform themselves deny the public their true franchise through illegal maneuvers and stoop to vicious tactics to achieve personal ends, it behooves our system of checks and balances to restore the faith of those who are sufficiently astute and concerned about the nation not be blinded by irrational, emotional political attachment. It is vital that honest, professional law enforcement personnel not be disillusioned because they find that indeed they are only pawns of politics. It is important that unprofessional officers not be encouraged by the oblique support of sanctioned misconduct. Few things can undercut respect for law more than the flaunting of political power, and certainly police recruitment is not aided by the misuse of such power.

PAWNS OF POWER

Some police departments are greatly influenced by monied interests and by right-wing groups. Usually there is adequate protection and immediate response in rich neighborhoods. Much the same can be said for upper-middle-class areas. An almost fawning type of behavior is said to be exhibited on occasion by even administrative officers on the police force when talking to wealthy individuals. Special treatment may be afforded these persons and their significant others. Drunken driving is overlooked, or the individual is shown extra courtesy and may be taken home in a patrol car. Generally this kind of service is not accorded minorities or the poor who are caught driving while intoxicated. Queries on this point bring the standard reply, "We are not a taxi service. We can't use our cars to take every drunk in town home." The point may be we well taken, but discrimination on the basis of race, color, or socioeconomic status certainly does not aid the police image.

When an officer "makes the mistake" of arresting an influential citizen, he is likely to see the individual's case dismissed or to see a very light fine imposed. The concerned officer who attempts to apply the law equally but fairly can become discouraged by VIP treatment of certain people and full use of the law against others. Some officers become angry and want to retaliate. As one put it, "When we go up there we have to knock on the door and when we are let in we have to be careful about the goddamned rug. We even have to take our caps off and hold them in our hands while we talk to those rich bastards. In a nigger neighborhood, we just kick the goddamned door down and walk in. Those fuckers know better than to start any shit with us."

It is highly possible that part of the harsh treatment received

by blacks is the result of pent-up anger that finds safe release
only in the black neighborhood. This is more than unequal treatment due to race because the behavior can be said to be more
a function of socioeconomic status than of race. Of course race
may play a role, but the poor white is treated no better than
blacks or Mexican-Americans in these instances.

An example was the witnessing of an arrest for intoxication
that was reported by a nurse. The victim, she said was too inebri-
ated to stand, but the officers beat him and seemed to get a particular glee from punching him in the genital area. When the young
woman tried to ask about this police action, she was threatened
with arrest for "interfering in an arrest." As she left the scene,
the officers were laughing at the drunken man as they literally
stuffed him in the patrol car. It is doubtful that the inebriate was
wealthy.

To be sure, not all officers pay homage to wealth, and some
are not intimidated by vested interest; but these men seem not to
advance rapidly on the force. Many officers who do not abuse citizens are seen as social workers and ridiculed by the "better" officers.

A real danger to police departments and a menace to society
is the far-right-wing influence in large numbers of police agencies.
In their study of the Denver police force, Bayley and Mendelsohn
reported a "tendency for policemen to be self-styled conservatives
more frequently than the majority general public."[5] William Parker,
former chief of the Los Angeles Police Department and acknowledged representative of police mentality, believed most patrolmen
to be "conservative, ultraconservative, and very right-wing."[6] Presidential aspirants Barry Goldwater and George Wallace drew significant support from the police. For example, although Denver went
to Lyndon Johnson by a two-to-one margin in the 1964 presidential
election, the Denver police supported Barry Goldwater 49 percent
to 47 percent.[7] The John Birch Society claims 500 members of
the New York City force.[8] With the cooperation of the Society,
Fred Grupp of Louisiana State University took a random sample
of Bircher membership. Of those reporting occupations, 3 percent
were policemen, a figure four times their proportion of the national
labor force.[9] In a California study cited by Lipset, "roughly ten
percent of the . . . policemen in practically every California city"
were members of the Ku Klux Klan.[10] The Black Legion, Father
Coughlin's Christian Front, and the American Protective Association have all drawn appreciable support from the police.

These groups can hardly be considered law-abiding, yet the
FBI discounts Klan activity. Once outlawed, this group has come

alive. Crosses are being burned again. Hate literature is distributed to school pupils and older students. Open membership drives have been undertaken. Weapons of all kinds are being stored. Newspaper accounts of the resurgence are frightening, but the FBI shrugs its shoulders and says, "We are watching them. There are only a few. They are not dangerous." One chief of police said, "They are not active. We have asked them, and they told us that they aren't doing anything." The same chief is said to have set an ambush for some black activists who were having a peaceful meeting to discuss a breakfast program for hungry children. As they left the meeting, they were fired upon and one was mortally wounded.

The FBI and other police agencies have spent long hours infiltrating among, harassing, and killing black activists who actually could pose little threat to anyone. First, these groups could not get the weaponry that members of white right-wing or left-wing organizations could obtain. Too many blacks are nonviolent for militant groups to recruit large numbers. The heavy infiltration by undercover agents, the long jail sentences assessed for minor infractions, and the deadly repressive police tactics actually have been ridiculous when measured against the permissive attitude taken toward radical and demonstrably dangerous right-wing groups.

In one Texas city members of the John Birch Society openly came to a police–community relations training program to "see what you are doing to *our* police." In Houston, Texas, John Birch Society members posed as police officers as an infiltration tactic to "protect" the police during the Houston Cooperative Crime Prevention Program. In addition, members of the Society passed out hate material in an endeavor to disrupt the meetings between community persons (of all races and socioeconomic backgrounds) and police officers. Designed to bring about a closer relationship between the average Houston citizen and the police, the meetings were being held in a tense time and under difficult circumstances. However, even admitted activists and admitted police racists were beginning to talk, and progress was being made. The Birchers almost succeeded in breaking the lines of communication that had been achieved. Even some of the announced bigots resented this intrusion. At one time a group of young black and white activists confronted a body of officers with strong language and emotion. The police administration and the officers threatened to terminate the meetings. Nothing was said about the disruptive John Birch Society action beyond, "It was uncalled for. They mean well, but you know how those things go." If stronger feelings were displayed, they were not in open evidence as they were any time Mexican-Americans, white "liberals," or concerned blacks raised searching questions or spoke out with passion about police misconduct.

The wife of a police cadet reported her husband as saying that he felt sick at the showing of John Birch films during secret training sessions. The films depicted Martin Luther King, Jr., as an avowed Communist and pointed to the danger of a black take-over of the country. The cadet told his wife that the distortions were of such nature that a weak-minded cadet might believe the propaganda, yet he was afraid to speak out against it.

One might speculate for a moment on the outcome should the Black Panthers show films to police cadets. What would happen if the Panthers or the SDS passed out literature to police officers at their training sessions? In fact, how welcome are Indians, Mexican-Americans, and/or black influences in police agencies beyond ineffective tokenism? The middle 1960s produced a kind of hysteria in white America beyond all reason, and the reaction of middle America may yet prove to be self-destructive. With its paranoia and ready backlash, middle America may do what no communist or fascist country could do to our nation. The ultraconservative right-wing influences in some police agencies may effect a total takeover and complete the forging of a police state in America. Such fears may seem ridiculous to a disinterested observer, but to the oppressed the danger appears real.

Unfortunately, too many law enforcement agencies are caught up in the same paranoia that permeates the atmosphere of extreme right-wing groups. They seem oblivious to the fact that members of these groups, and others who are hate mongers, actually espouse the philosophy of Adolf Hitler. They can be heard saying his exact words:

> The streets of our country are in turmoil. The universities
> are filled with students rebelling and rioting. Communists
> are seeking to destroy our country. Russia is threatening us
> with her might and the republic is in danger. Yes, danger
> from within and without. We need law and order. (Adolf
> Hitler, 1932)[11]

The bumper sticker "America: Love It or Leave It" echoes the same blind, unquestioning rhetoric of the fanatic Nazi and indicates a similar mentality. It leaves no middle ground for "America: If You Love Her, Help Mend Her Ills." This is not to demean a country or to be unpatriotic. Our greatest statesmen and our most patriotic heroes were constantly seeking means to improve an imperfect democracy. They recognized that any great undertaking would have weaknesses and any great political philosophy would need unremitting scrutiny. But these were great minds. Although bumper stickers are on the wane, some people still raise questions about the feelings and attitudes that gave rise to them.

It may be that the antiminority, antipoor mood of the country during the late 1960s set the direction or reinforced the direction of our police authority. Police were encouraged to use "any means necessary" to curb even peaceful demonstrations. Many of the "means necessary" will go down in historical infamy. The faces of police officers filled with hate and the pictures of police dogs being permitted to chew at the stomach and groin of restrained youth will remain emblazoned on the mind of America. Helpless black women and children photographed while being brutalized by their "protectors" should have tweaked the conscience of middle America. If they did, the distress was short lived. Even the media, attempting to reflect the overreaction on reverse violence, were exposed to verbal attack by our former vice-president and physical attack by law enforcement agencies. A larger segment of the society applauded the federal government for its inactivity or its echoing of the infamous cry for "law and order." There was no mention of justice. Throughout, the police were on the front lines and were used as "cannon fodder."

The political consciousness of law enforcement officers (that had seemed to lie dormant except for concern with pay raises and working conditions), awakened precipitously by the sounds of social change, was now ready for direct political involvement in response to the mood of the country. The entry into direct political action was abrupt and successful. The Minneapolis story is a fair reflection of what really happened among police:

> The Minneapolis experience is instructive. The police in that city were prepared to exploit the law and order mood of the community in the mayoral campaign of 1969. They were prepared because, over a sustained period of time, they had organized politically and had developed requisite political skills. Thus equipped, they went out and captured the most politically significant office that makes law enforcement policy in the city.
>
> There were, of course, many factors that accounted for the mayoral victory of a policeman in Minneapolis: the fertile territory for a law and order appeal among the city's high proportion of white working-class and elderly residents, the impact of black and student disorders at home and across

the nation, a serious split in the city's Democratic-Farmer-Labor Party, and the ineffective campaigning of the Republican candidate.[12]

The necessary ingredients for a successful campaign were there.

A WAY OUT

Direct involvement in politics and the political activism of police seemed one way to change their image or to garner the power to maintain their image without fear. The politcial area might solve for them the problems of unrealistic external demand and shaky professional prestige.

> Studies of occupational prestige over the past decade showed low ranking for the police—47th and 54th out of 90 listed occupations. Policemen ranked beneath machinists or undertakers in one survey; they tied with railroad conductors in another.[13]

Status is very important to professionals. Even groups within a profession vie for status. The history of law enforcement makes prestige a rare commodity for a police officer except among his peers. The image of the officer as a dimwit who is long on brawn and short on brain still haunts the profession. Until recently, the lack of college-trained police served to validate in the widespread attitude that the level of intelligence among policemen was far below that found in many other occupations. Sheriff departments, constables, and police in rural areas still bear the stigma of being seen as stupid.

Politics looked like a way out—especially for chiefs of police. They saw elected officials who could boast of little more than selling ax handles to members of mobs or who came into office on antiblack, antipoor, and antiyouth platforms. Yet these men wielded power once they were in office. Riding the crest of a popular, emotional wave seemed more important than dealing with fundamental issues. The mood of the country made the election of any law-and-order candidate a certainty. Who could be more qualified than a former police officer? Already steeped in conservatism, would he not appeal to an ultraconservative electorate? Given these odds and this knowledge, it was logical that individuals who at one time were supposed to be nonpolitical would enter the political ring with gusto. Here was a chance for status and for power. The whole idea of equality and justice paled into insignificance as power and prestige became more and more the political ideal. The pawns of politics and of power were finding a way to *be* the politicians and to *be* the power. The sad fact here is that even in victory the police officer was still a pawn. However, for his consolation, he was in a position now to exert *some* direct power. Now *he* is the politician. It remains to be seen whether *justice* and *equality* follow.

The police officer has a right, as a citizen, to political office. Nonetheless, as with any other citizen, his motivation and his qualifications to serve should be of major concern to the voting public. The difference between good government and bad government is the difference between the individual who goes into office for personal power and/or vindictive reasons and the official who seeks to *serve* the best interests of his public. This is the case whether the candidate is a chief of police or a political science major.

The law enforcement person who wins public office faces his "minority status" once more. Like the Negro, Mexican-American, or American Indian, he must bear closer observation and harsher criticism than other officeholders. When he is found guilty of breaking the law—before *or* after his election—public confidence in any police candidate is shaken, and the situation tends to have a deleterious effect upon the total political process. Evidence of this condition is the public apathy displayed at the polls. Even the presidential election of 1972 was more a landslide for apathy than a mandate from the people. The trend has continued in most recent elections. Lack of confidence in politicians has reached a new high, and the increased political activity of police as a body (particularly as an ultraconservative group) poses a real danger to them in terms of public support. Were law enforcement relatively free of political influence and if politicians could neither coerce nor threaten law enforcement officers, at least one problem of and for police officers would be solved. Favor could not court favor, and the average citizen would not be liable to two powerful forces in his life and the interplay between them.

No one should be more aware of this crunch than the law enforcement officer. His election could greatly reduce political and power influences within police departments. But if his primary reason for election is the substitution of just another individual whose goals and controls rest with the vested interests of law enforcement, our political condition will only have moved—not changed. If the pawn, once in power, becomes the oppressor and others become pawns, things will still be really the same. It is to be hoped that law enforcement officers who go into active politics and who seek public office will use their experience and influence to strengthen our system of justice and to take the unfair pressures off their fellows.

Law enforcement personnel and the general public must admit to themselves the danger of too much power in the hands of any individual or any group. Tunnel vision that has focused only on the suppression of minorities and the poor must be corrected. Law enforcement agencies and citizenry must not only resist manipulation but assure freedom of law enforcement from *any* special interest—and most particularly extremist groups of *any* persuasion. We must be equally vigilant that powerful individuals or groups do not overly influence or control police conduct. All Americans must have the right to *equal* treatment under the law. That is possible only when law enforcement functions as a free agent, guided and directed by an intelligent electorate that sets guidelines but *permits* proper police prerogative, free of unscrupulous political or vested power intervention.

CHAPTER 8

PROBLEMS OF TRAINING
AND
SUPERVISION

If police departments are a critical variable in defining the character and functioning of American society, then the training and supervision of lawmen assumes special significance. As of 1966 only 50 of the 40,000 law enforcement agencies in the United States were agencies of the federal government.[1] State agencies accounted for an additional 200.[2] Thus 39,750 police agencies are responsible to the villages or cities where they work.[3]

As previously noted, this administrative dispersal largely accounts for the variety of local police forces. If Berkeley differs from Atlanta, their respective police departments are likely to differ too—in philosophy, in methodology, in politics. What is true of policemen in Boston may not be true of their Austin counterparts.

We have also noted, however, some commonalities: the political nature of police, the implicit discretion required of officers, the inherent contradictions of their work. Police forces are essentially closed systems; one moves up through the ranks, thereby minimizing the likelihood of diverse experiences or viewpoints.

Unfortunately, an excellent patrolman may make a poor administrator and vice versa. The police system is a meritocracy, and meritocracies can compromise the worker's effectiveness by forcing him either to neglect or to overzealously pursue his duty in the hope of being promoted. Transfers may also negate talents.

To qualify as a police candidate, one must comply with certain standard requirements—that is, be 21 years of age or older, be a citizen of the United States, and possess a twelfth-grade education or better. It is generally necessary to pass a written test, a physical examination, and an oral interview. The candidate cannot have been convicted of a felony, and he is subject to an exhaustive scrutiny of his moral character. The latter stipulation, while sometimes questionable in its rigorous application as it relates to white candidates, serves as an obstacle to political activists and to members of racial minorities who might have minor arrest records. Rates of acceptance are low: 15 percent in New York, 6 percent in Tucson, 5 percent in Berkeley, and 4 percent in Los Angeles during a 12-year period beginning in 1950.[4]

Who are the police forces in the United States?

> The average Southern policeman is a promoted poor white
> with a legal sanction to use a weapon. His social heritage
> has taught him to despise the Negroes, and he has had
> little education which could have changed him.[5]

> Working-class background, high-school education or less,
> average intelligence, cautious personality—these are the typi-
> cal features of the modern police recruit. Only in his superior
> physical endowment does he stand above the crowd.[6]

The Denver study found the average policeman to be white, Protestant, married, and the father of two or three children. While minorities constituted 22 percent of the general population, they represented 5 percent of the police force.[7] Although the police had a higher educational level than the population as a whole, fewer proportionately were college graduates.

Given the complexity and seriousness of their jobs, policemen have a history of being woefully undertrained (see Table 3). Sometimes training is nil. Eighteen percent of all municipal police departments fail to provide *any* training. As will be pointed out, this situation is gradually being remedied in many cities.

> Today, about one-quarter of all cities and half of the small
> towns still do nothing to train new recruits, unless it is to
> refer them to the Ten Commandments. Only a small minority
> of agencies providing training do so upon entry; the vast
> majority send new men out on the street immediately and
> train them—if at all—"as soon as possible" within their first
> year.

> Once an officer has passed the recruit stage, he is unlikely
> to receive further training to maintain or improve his general
> competence or to qualify him for specialized assignment or

TABLE 3
MEDIAN MINIMUM TRAINING HOURS

LINE OF WORK	NUMBER OF HOURS
Physicians	11,000
Embalmers	5,000
Barbers	4,000
Beauticians	1,200
Policemen	less than 200

SOURCE: Seymour Martin Lipset, "Why Cops Hate Liberals—and Vice Versa," *Atlantic Monthly*, vol. 223, March 1969, p. 83. Copyright © 1969, by The Atlantic Monthly Company, Boston, Mass. Reprinted with permission.
NOTE: The vast majority of policemen begin carrying guns and enforcing the law with less than five weeks' training of any kind.

promotion. Few departments conduct systematic inservice training for all personnel, and fewer still provide formal management training for those entrusted with administrative and supervisory responsibilities.[8]

Such inadequacies in training can handicap the officer in dealing with his routine duties involving personal interaction with citizens, as well as in the more sensitive situations.

It is rarely recognized that the conduct of police may be related in a fundamental way to the character and goals of the institution itself—the duties police are called upon to perform, associated with the assumptions of the system of legal justice—and that it may not be men who are good or bad, so much as the premises and design of the system in which they find themselves.[9]

Inadequate training results in unqualified officers providing inadequate police service. "A significant percentage of the men on any force are not suited to meet the responsibilities of modern law enforcement."[10]

Studies of police in New York City and Denver did not reveal that police officers are any more authoritarian than members of the dominant population. However, "there is a social process at work within the police system that precipitates the most authoritarian type into the authoritarian role at the lowest level of the hierarchy, pounding the beat."[11] Thus the opportunities for misunderstanding, for conflict, and for abuse are increased.

Standards to which law enforcement agents are urged to adhere are quite idealistic. Typical is the Law Enforcement Code of Ethics, originally adopted in 1956 by the California Peace Officers Association and since embraced by national police organizations.

> AS A LAW ENFORCEMENT OFFICER my fundamental duty is to mankind; to safeguard lives and property; to protect the innocent against deception, the weak against oppression and intimidation, and the peaceful against violence and disorder; to respect the CONSTITUTIONAL rights of all men to liberty, equality and justice.
>
> I will keep my private life unsullied as an example to all; maintain courageous calm in the face of danger, scorn, or ridicule; develop self-restraint; and be constantly mindful of the welfare of others. I will be exemplary in obeying the laws of the land and the regulations of my department. Whatever I see or hear of a confidential nature, or that is confided in me in my official capacity, will be kept secret unless revelation is necessary in the performance of my duty.
>
> I will never act officiously or permit personal feelings, prejudices, animosities or friendships to influence my decisions. With no compromise for crime and with relentless prosecution of criminals, I will enforce the law courteously and appropriately without fear or favor, malice or ill-will, never employing unnecessary force or violence and never accepting gratuities. I RECOGNIZE the badge of my office as a symbol of public faith, and I accept it as a public trust to be held so long as I am true to the ethics of the police service. I will constantly strive to achieve these objectives and ideals, dedicating myself before God to my chosen profession—LAW ENFORCEMENT.[12]

Not dissimilar is the FBI Pledge:

> Humbly recognizing the responsibilities entrusted to me, I do vow that I shall always consider the high calling of law enforcement to be an honorable profession, the duties of which are recognized by me as both an art and a science. . . .
>
> I am aware of the serious responsibilities of my office and in the performance of my duties, I shall, as a *minister*, seek to supply comfort, advice, and aid to those who may be in need of such benefits; as a *soldier*, I shall wage vigorous

warfare against the enemies of my country, of its laws, and
of its principles; and as a *physician,* I shall seek to eliminate
the criminal parasite which preys upon our social order and
to strengthen the lawful processes of our body politic. I shall
strive to be both a *teacher* and a *pupil* in the art and science
of law enforcement. As a *lawyer,* I shall acquire due knowledge of the laws of my domain and seek to preserve and
maintain the majesty and dignity of the law; as a *scientist,*
it will be my endeavor to learn all pertinent truth about accu-
sations and complaints which come to my lawful knowledge;
as an *artist,* I shall seek to use my skill for the purpose of
making each assignment a masterpiece; as a *neighbor,* I shall
bear an attitude of true friendship and courteous respect to
all citizens; and as an *officer,* I shall always be loyal to my
duty, my organization and my country. [Italics added.][13]

Unfortunately, these grandiose exhortations, rather than encouraging professionalism, seem to promote cynicism. The average recruit's
background, training, and on-the-job experiences tend to refute
such niceties.

One of the major variances associated with police work has
been the method of training. Police appointments are no longer
solely the result of political patronage. Increasing emphasis on
college education and the use of civil service examinations are
slowly changing the character of various departments.

The emphasis in college education for police departs sharply
from training offered in the traditional police academy. The
college-educated police officer studies such subjects as causes
of crime and deviant behavior, the psychology of youthful
and adult offenders, minority group relations, urban sociology,
social problems, probation and parole supervision, constitutional law, and community relations. He is also enrolled in
courses in statistics, advanced management techniques, com-
puter science, and research methods.

Police academy training, which has traditionally introduced
the new officer to accident investigation, use of firearms, report
writing, and laws of arrest and of search and seizure, will
continue. . . .

The curricula for in-service police training places emphasis
on "how to do" police work; the education offered in colleges
and universities, on the other hand, enables the officer to
recognize the social and psychological significance of what
he does. Police authorities believe that ideally an officer should

first receive an education, because training goals can then
be achieved with greater ease.[14]

The most significant factor influencing police roles is the
dichotomy between law enforcement and order maintenance.

> . . . The former involves a violation of a law in which only
> guilt need be assessed; the latter, though it often entails a
> legal infraction, involves in addition a dispute in which the
> law must be interpreted, standards of right conduct deter-
> mined, and blame assigned.[15]

Law enforcement implies victimization; arrests are sought, if not
secured. Questions of enforcement require the officer to compare
behavior with a statute. Departments emphasizing enforcement are
characterized by high rates of arrests and ticketing, by a promotion
system based on arrest records, and by a desired maximization
of technology. Punitive standards accompanying this interpretation
of police responsibility generate a large volume of contact with
the citizenry. Consequently, while harassment and other forms of
official abuse may be proportionately lower within a department
stressing enforcement instead of maintenance, the number of such
incidents is higher in absolute terms within an enforcement-con-
scious force.

Enforcement also presumes a substantial amount of police-
citizen cooperation, as the public must make the policeman aware
of violations except in those rare instances in which the officer
himself sees the law broken. Contrary to the image fostered by
the media, most police activity is not dramatic investigations and
manhunts. Enforcement of criminal law commands less than 30
percent of the working time of uniformed police in their working
areas.[16] Only one-third of police radio calls involve criminal matters
potentially warranting arrest, which in turn occurs in only about
5 percent of the instances.[17] Only one-fifth of one percent of those
arrested are charged with homicide; less than 10 percent of all
arrested are charged with any of the seven serious offenses on
the FBI Crime Index.[18] In Denver, approximately two-thirds of
the officers interviewed said that not more than 9 percent of their
contacts resulted in either arrest or citation.[19]

Thus police work is mainly concerned with the maintaining
of order, entailing "handling of disputes in which only two or
three people participate and which arise out of personal misconduct, not racial or class grievances."[20] Nonetheless, order maintenance may expose the policeman to physical danger, as well as
forcing him to deal with a situation in which the laws are not

specifically applicable and in which he must determine what constitutes "public order" and to what extent, if any, it has been violated.

Public cooperation is even more essential in order maintenance than in the area of law enforcement. Police forces emphasizing maintenance tend to seek control, rather than elimination, of crime, and to judge infractions in terms of immediate and personal consequences. Unlike enforcement-geared departments, maintenance forces do not stress a policeman's arrest record and have a less adversary relationship with the public, being more sensitive to personality and political variables. Although order maintenance constitutes a substantial part of police work, it is also a neglected one.

> The organization of police departments and the training of policemen are focused almost entirely on the apprehension and prosecution of criminals. What a policeman does, or should do, instead of making an arrest or in order to avoid making an arrest, or in a situation in which he may not make an arrest, is rarely discussed. The peacekeeping and service activities, which consume the majority of police time, receive too little consideration.[21]

Police may frequently facilitate order maintenance through nonintervention. This enforcement-maintenance dichotomy is a crucial one in terms of police policy. Law enforcement presupposes specialization, a concern with technology, specific codes and procedures, firm hierarchical authority, and close surveillance of the public by the policing agents. Order maintenance, however, implies decentralization, reliance on cooperative police-public interaction rather than technology, flexible procedural policies, and even a degree of "bossism." The resolution of the dilemma of whether a policeman can be both a professional enforcer and a public servant will to a large extent determine the character of American society in the immediate future.

Many officers are shuttled from selection to training to their beat without adequate allowance for the peculiar problems and contradictions their work entails. Scant attention, if any, is given the service aspect of police work, and psychological aids are ignored. All too frequently, psychological and legal complexities of the policeman's job are neglected in the rush to get him into uniform and onto the street. The International Chiefs of Police in 1968 conducted a study that showed only 41 of 162 major law enforcement agencies in the United States administered psychological tests to applicants; not even personal interviews were conducted by six of the agencies.[22]

Although numerous corporations administer psychological tests to potential employees—employees who will staff nonsensitive and noncontroversial positions—few police departments bother to psychologically screen applicants. Yet policemen will daily deal with people in a variety of situations, some of which may result in violence.

Psychological as well as physical health is essential to a police officer. Therefore, psychological screening should be an initial provision. A psychological profile could be maintained to detect changes which can affect the officer's performance of duties. This would benefit both the policeman and the citizens with whom he deals by monitoring the officer's psychological health.

Regardless of how one views the police—as saviors or oppressors—their existence and their situation represent objective conditions which should be understood.

The psychological health of the junior law enforcement officer is as much an extension of the psychological welfare of the command or senior officer as it is a result of his general milieu. To be explicit, many officers become a carbon copy of their superior officer. Reports from some recently commissioned officers reflect excellent training and supervision. They tell of assistance given to citizens (typical of "Adam-12" or similar shows), they point to "good" arrests, they reveal the use of good judgment, and they cite occasions on which the necessary and optimum use of force was displayed without brutality. These officers told of mistakes made by their superiors, but they spoke also with pride about the courage of their command officers who openly acknowledged error and had the fortitude to rectify the mistake or to apologize.

Unfortunately there were those whose stories were just the opposite. Following a training session, a young patrolman said, "What do you do when the sergeant who rates you and who actually has your future in his hands makes you do things that you don't want to do?" He told of an occasion when the command officer saw a black man walking along the street and said, "Pull over! I want to show you something." When the car was stopped, he called the black over to the car and verbally abused the man. When he had finished he said to the young officer, "That's the way you have to treat niggers. Did you see the respect I got? He has several stitches in his head where I had to teach him some manners one night. He won't forget that! Let's go see if we can find some nigger whores." The young officer told of having to physically abuse winos, blacks, Mexican-Americans, and others who probably would not report the incidents. The frustrating statement from this new police officer was, "You know, I still don't

like to do that but *it comes easy for me now.* I guess I'm telling
you because I still don't think it's right." Other men described
other types of unprofessional acts demanded by hardened, cynical
supervisors. None of these men complained, for fear of reprisal.
This may not be a common practice (although it was said to be
in the particular department), but *one* such supervisor is too costly
to *any* police department.

In still another situation, the individual riding with a police
officer reported an incident in which a little black girl smiled and
waved at the passing patrol car. She said, "Hello, Mr. Policeman."
Under his breath the officer replied (while waving and smiling),
"Hello, little nigger!" Countless incidents of undue harassment,
overreaction, and bigotry would seem to indicate something to
a training officer.

Despite the continuing complaints against some police officers,
only token attention to the matter is given in their training sessions.
Police-citizen relationships (particularly involving minority groups
and the poor) keep on being abrasive. Each time they appear
to be improving, a new incident fans the flames of discontent.
Evidently "Where there's smoke, there's fire" is a truism *except*
in the area of complaints against police officers. Policemen in pursuit of their duties must not be harassed. They must not have
their effectiveness limited by psychological assault in the form of
complaints against them. At the same time, supervisors and chiefs
of police must not let a misdirected form of police "loyalty" prevent
them from vigorously urging proper professional conduct among
officers. Collusion seems to be common in the law enforcement
field, particularly as it relates to misconduct.

> Two principal characteristics emerge from this group loyalty:
> suspicion and hostility directed at any outside interference
> with the department. This mixture of hostility and pride has
> created what the Commission has found to be the most serious
> roadblock to a rational attack upon police corruption: a stub-
> born refusal at all levels of the department to acknowledge
> that a serious problem exists.

Chiefs of police feel bound to mouth platitudes and make
loud pronouncements about departmental policy as relates to police
misconduct, while at the same time strongly defending men who
they *know* are wrong. A "slap on the wrist" is a common response
to a proved complaint. Suspension for a few days is seen as harsh
punishment for more serious acts against the citizen. Dismissal
is used only in the most extreme cases and is carried out in a

manner "not to hurt the man." Seldom is he unable to go to another police department and get hired at once. Almost never is he criminally prosecuted for the same assaultive behavior for which an ordinary citizen would be jailed—sometimes without bond. The record of nonpunishment or light punishment for law enforcement officers involved in murders of civil rights demonstrators (*peaceful* demonstrators) attests to this assertion. The current record is little better. Somewhere training and supervision need reevaluating.

It is incongruous that a large number of officers in a Texas city can consider one part of the city (the larger black and Mexican-American community) "Vietnam"; can openly call it that; can respond to simple calls *en masse* (seven and eight patrol cars)— and all this not be known to their command officers. It looks as if police cadets are *taught* to suspect and to be afraid of nonwhite minority groups. Stop-and-frisk, stop-and-search, and other similar procedures are proper and necessary, but their indiscriminate use against minority target groups is unconscionable. Proper training (or more appropriately, proper *education*) should reduce the incidence of many unethical practices. Granted that numerous departments across the country are engaged in upgrading but this fact should not diminish our thrust everywhere for better training and supervision.

Of course chiefs of police cannot closely supervise *all* command officers at the same time. Nor can supervisors be at the scene of every police action. Nonetheless, proper education and training are reflected in other areas of police action. Why not the same careful, professional, and ethical reflection of education for optimum community relations? It is obvious that white-black relations resulting from years of unmitigated white racism and black resistance have been the most dangerous divisive factor in our country. The recent history of documented police action against blacks has not improved things, despite warnings, solicitations, petitions, and imploration from many sectors regarding police violence against minorities—and more especially blacks. "For a year later, we are a year closer to being two societies, black and white, increasingly separated and scarcely less unequal."[23] The situation remains a joke in some departments, and some officers are anxious for a showdown. Surely supervisors must know about their attitude. Many command officers pass this attitude to younger officers.

Somewhere in the curriculum stress must be placed upon the need for officers to realize that their conduct at all times is under scrutiny. Somewhere in the curriculum it must be emphasized that the sensitivity of the police role and the responsibility of the police profession will not tolerate behavior that tarnishes a desirable law enforcement image. If this lesson is taught at all, it is certainly not well learned; the student apparently knows that it is of lesser importance than his "taking charge." In fact, he seems to feel assured that only in cases of gross, obvious unprofessionalism with respect to minorities will he be disciplined.

Evidently departments do not make studies of time spent using surveillance tactics and repressive measures against minorities and the poor. They do not evaluate this time in terms of the product and to ascertain how at least *some* of the time might be more efficiently spent. Maybe academies need updating in the behavioral sciences to equal their courses in weaponry and other technical training. The boredom on the faces of too many cadets during human relations training seminars and the mockery made of this phase of training indicate its lack of impact and lack of real concern. What academies have to learn is that repressive measures are only temporary and cannot contain a people forever. Society progresses by cooperative endeavor, not by force or farce.

Police should have learned this lesson during the upheavals of the 1960s. Many an officer had his "mind blown" and lost complete control because he couldn't handle psychological pressure exerted by sophisticated college youth. Except for the more professionally trained and socially skilled police officer, it is doubtful still that the average policeman is sufficiently psychologically integrated to withstand verbal attack.

There is abundant evidence that police are well trained in the use of weapons, criminal psychology, and techniques of crime fighting and/or prevention. A growing body of evidence supports concerns about the strength of the psychological integration of most police officers.

Attempts by behavioral scientists to cooperate with and to help police departments have been met with contempt, suspicion, or outright hostility. In a meeting of the International Chiefs of Police, a very progressive chief told a group of experienced police behavioral scientists that he dared not suggest to other chiefs of police that they take advantage of the behavioral science resources within that room. Times were changing, he said, and the day was coming when police and social scientists would work together (as they were working in his department), but not for a few years. In fact, many police associations show a real paranoia about social scientists.

This indictment can be annulled through intelligent law enforcement leadership. The old order must change. Even organized crime has a high degree of sophistication. The use of new equipment is only a partial answer. Police must begin to understand human behavior. The criminal is no longer the stereotyped dimwit or the slick gangster. He is the astute politician. He is the above-average student. He is a preadolescent. He is versed in law. He fits the spectrum of society, and his criminal acts defy definition. Or he is a psychotic killer.

Problems of supervision and training will not be solved until the interpersonal and training problems within departments are honestly faced. They will not be solved until police agencies stop being closed and closed-minded societies open themselves to persons who want to support their activities with new expertise. New and growing demands require widened learning experiences for the police officer, who certainly works against tremendous odds.

In some areas strong cultural patterns exist and languages other than English are spoken. Particularly is this the case in the Southwest and some sections of California, where the Spanish tongue is common. Police departments make wide use of their Mexican-American personnel in certain situations, but they do not really try to prepare their Anglo officers for general contact with Spanish-speaking persons. Some knowledge of Spanish (for maximum practical use) and a basic understanding of Mexican-American culture should be a requirement in police academies. Solutions to problems related to cultural or language differences should not be left to chance. Police serve a pluralistic and multicultural society. Where the differences are specific, equal protection is a myth if a means of affording equal understanding is not provided. The initiative belongs to the law enforcement training agency. Fortunately, departments are beginning to face this issue and to offer courses to remedy the shortcoming.

Training and supervision for the sensitive but demanding responsibility of becoming a law enforcement officer are by nature exceedingly difficult. Improper training or improper supervision can cost a police officer his life and can result in lifetime guilt for an instructor or supervisor. Only law enforcement personnel completely understand the rigors of training and the reasons for stringent rules of conduct. Yet, until that training and that education succeed in producing much larger numbers of honest, impartial, dedicated men and women, society as a whole will continue to be short-changed.

Scientific studies of all aspects of education and training by *qualified* outside agencies should be permitted. These agencies should work hand in hand with the police establishment to continue improving training and supervision in order to assure a police professionalism of which even the layman can be proud. America owes this to her citizens.

CHAPTER 9

THE CRITICAL NEED FOR PUBLIC UNDERSTANDING AND SUPPORT

PRESSURES FROM SOCIETY

Most of us tend to take law enforcement for granted. Seldom is the policeman viewed as having the same desires, worries, and personal problems as the rest of us. Many police officers have rightly complained that the general public sees them as inhuman or as robots. For example, one citizen said of police officers, "They only see the world through their windshields. They don't know what it's like to relate to people as human beings. They never get close to people. They are just like robots."

There is no doubt that a large number of us fail to see the human side of law enforcement persons. We are blind to the fact that they are used by others. Politicians sometimes use them as footballs and city councilmen may use them as footstools. Parents use them to frighten their children into behaving in a desired manner. Later it is difficult to change this ogre into a helping person, and parents don't understand why their children withdraw from policemen.

The officer is often the victim of a whim. He is wanted only when needed. He is someone to avoid, to fear, to hold in suspicion, or—according to your politics—to kill. This unthinking, insensitive attitude of the public is a real ally to criminality. The officer has little energy left to combat crime or criminality when much of it is constantly used up in mutually hostile feelings between him and the average citizen. Even the lack of cooperation by John Q. Public can result in emotional drain on the part of the officer who needs information in order to fulfill his duty to protect that same Mr. Public.

Middle America has created an even worse kind of pressure for the average police officer. Its overreaction to beards, long hair, blackness, brownness, and the like, is forced upon the law enforcement person, whose responsibility it is to carry out the will of society. Thus he has had to spend much time at least harassing unarmed dissidents who aside from getting their greatest kick out of heckling "pigs" may have been relatively harmless. On the other hand, he faced the possibility that these individuals were only posing as hippies, being really criminals in disguise. A serious lack of education and training prevented many officers from differentiating among those who "looked alike." Consequently, they drew ire and hatred from persons who, though "different," were in no way a threat to anything but the status quo in terms of dress and grooming. Had society not placed such pressures upon the police officer, he might have been able to handle the situation expeditiously. But he found himself forced to react quickly and often without thought in order to avoid extreme criticism from the members of a society whose values he was supposed to protect.

Society seems much more anxious to use the full resources of the police department to rouse the Black Panthers, political dissidents, hippies, and left-wing groups than to use them against organized criminal activity. Note the contradiction in the fact that when political activists and others used violent means to achieve their ends, this violence was quickly and sometimes overzealously met; but when right-wing groups and hard hats behaved in a violent manner, they found little resistance from the police. Indeed, there is evidence that in at least one instance the police stood by while the hard hats waded into a group of unarmed people and literally beat some of them to the ground.

Middle Americans did not mind violence if it obtained their ultraconservative or reactionary end, and they did not want the police to interfere with this kind of violence. The professional officer was therefore put in an ambiguous situation because to him violence was violence no matter who was the perpetrator. Yet he found himself condemned if he attempted to intervene in one kind of violence but severely chastised if he didn't react swiftly and strongly to the violence from another side. These kinds of social demands placed the police officer in an untenable position. Sworn to uphold the law *impartially* and without exception, he found himself the whipping boy of the electorate and the scapegoat for the politically and financially powerful. He could not uphold the law equally whether confronting the violent left or the violent right. He found himself misused by the powerful and subsequently mistrusted by the powerless.

This dilemma is at least partially the fault of those of us who invest little or nothing in support of law enforcement. Our interest in law enforcement is only that the police officer be there immediately when we need him. Otherwise we would rather not see him. We have left his support, until recently, almost totally to vested interest groups.

Many citizens talk about our moving toward a police state but they are not sufficiently alarmed to get involved. They seem to feel that as long as they are "law-abiding" they have nothing to fear. To some the giving up of individual rights is small pay for the "comfort of noninvolvement" or the "security of a safe society." They are unaware of the danger that impends. When individual rights are given up, involvement in government is refused—particularly in the area of criminal justice.

Another frustration for the professional policeman is the recent behavior of "law-abiding citizens." Until a law-abiding community abides by the law in deed rather than in slogans, the officer's job remains emotionally exhausting. Law-abiding citizens attacked little black children en route to school. Law-abiding citizens burned buses. Law-abiding citizens threatened, harassed, and attacked minority families attempting to move to a home at the site of their choice, which sometimes happened to be in an all-white neighborhood. Law-abiding citizens formed vigilante groups. Patriotic, law-abiding citizens print and distribute hate literature. Law-abiding citizens deny certain segments of our community their rights to life, liberty, and the pursuit of happiness guaranteed by the Constitution. Such a state of affairs should not pose a problem in the area of police prerogative, but it does. No matter how much he abhors what is happening, somehow he has been trained that this is the will of the majority and it is his responsibility to deal with the problem as if it were a "delicate situation" rather than a crime.

At the same time he is dealing with criminal activity on the part of the far right, he must face criminal activity on the part of the far left. He is caught between the truly concerned white citizen who is not a member of an extremist group and the truly concerned black person who is not a member of an extremist group. And there are numerous groups all along the spectrum, each demanding that he take sides with it. If the general public has any idea of the tremendous frustration the officer feels it shows little evidence of willingness to become sufficiently involved in this problem to help him.

Until individuals who really believe in the democratic principles upon which our government was founded start to scrutinize critically the agencies developed to guarantee liberty and justice for all, the untenable position of the police officer will make liberty and justice for all, including himself, an extremely difficult goal.

ADMINISTRATIVE PRESSURES

Administrative inconsistencies can be especially frustrating. For example, radar units are reported to be disallowed in some sections of town. "The word is handed down and we don't go out there because we caught some old boy and he squawked. Next thing we knew we were told, 'Don't go out there any more.'" Or some people are not to receive tickets for minor offenses. None of this circumspection is in the rule book. It is a matter of discretion. But it does put the police officer in a bind. Ticket quotas are major fund-raising devices in some cities—a policy that is vigorously denied by officials but acknowledged by the officers. Promotions or good records may be based on the "two a day," and punishment may follow resistance to this course of action. Fund-raising projects and the like may become an unofficial responsibility in some departments.

Like other minorities, the police are in a power relationship. The ire of a councilman can be costly to an officer, but he has no more recourse in real terms than does the Mexican-American against an unscrupulous Texas Ranger. The same may obtain with a state official. In such situations the administrative response is, "You should have known better." Carrying out the law while not carrying out the law is not a simple task.

The discrepancy between the hierarchical position of the police officer in his militaristic organizational chart and his *actual* position leaves him constantly vulnerable with no viable recourse for personal cause. He must find some acceptable release for resentment caused by "I had to make that damned quota. Who gets it? Some poor black or Mexican-American fucker who makes an honest mistake but is technically wrong! I gotta issue that poor son of a bitch a ticket while I look at his six or seven kids and know goddamn well the cost of this ticket will take food out the mouths of those kids! In the meantime Mr. Rich Bitch cracks all kinds of laws and I can't touch his ass!" The anger and frustration are there, but the police officer is not permitted the luxury of releasing it in the most appropriate and direct way. Political whim can be the ill wind that blows him no good, but his is not to question. His is to do, and often he dies. This is police reality.

Administrative pressures and the types of these pressures will vary from department to department, but they are a constant mean-ace to police personnel. Sometimes the whole idea becomes one of survival. The idealistic officers suffer the most from undue or unfair administrative practices. However, like the beleaguered Christian minister who remains in an anti-Christian climate in his church, the officer with ideals remains on the force "because he must." Just as there is always police prerogative, there has to be administrative prerogative—but it should always be with the law.

PERSONAL PRESSURES

The nature of his job makes it difficult for the policeman to com-municate with those outside the ranks. Sometimes this inability to communicate or lack of communication reaches into the fam-ily structure. What do you tell your family? How much do you tell your family? What can you share? What can you not afford to share? The officer has to deal with these kinds of questions, knowing that no matter how accepting, the members of the family must find it hard to tolerate his treating them with reserve. Again like other minorities, the police are a visible element in the societal context, and as their visibility level rises in a hostile environment, the probability of conflict increases. Possibily the sharpest personal pain felt by him results from what happens to his family. How often have other children refused to play with an officer's child? How many times have the children of the cop on the block been ostracized or intimidated? If a policeman's family is not overtly ostracized, it may nevertheless be seen as "different," a view which can enable one to adopt prejudicial attitudes without being "prejudiced." An officier's wife and children may suffer verbal insults and unintentional slights. Sometimes the unintended hurt is the cruelest of all. To most of us, a policeman's life doesn't seem so hard—riding around in a car and writing out tickets. If few of us have ever seen the results of a violent crime, perhaps even fewer of us have seen a policeman bleed.

Such attitudes soon make an officer and his family feel mis-understood and unappreciated. Like any minority group under sim-ilar pressures, the police community withdraws into itself. The result is a kind of unhealthy paranoia and restricted socialization. As a result of constant verbal abuse (even in the form of painful jokes), "the isolation process takes just about a year to draw a circle around most any police family."[1]

Just as a police officer may stereotype a black youth as disre-spectful or a longhair as a doper, cynical citizens may pigeonhole a policeman as a licensed thug too dumb to get a better job but smart enough to get on the take. It is in this area that the police officer should be most sensitive to the pain experienced by other minority groups. It is much easier for him to take personal insults or even assaults than to see his family suffer and find himself helpless.

Inadequate salaries force some officers to moonlight. This situation is especially harmful because it allows a policeman to spend even less time with his family and because the energy expended in the other job may adversely affect the performance of his police duties. Although salaries are increasing, they are far from ideal.

> Median starting salaries for patrolmen range from $6,607 in smaller communities to $7,043 in cities of 250,000–500,000. By regions, they range from $5,214 in the South to $7,458 in the West. Maximums for patrolmen are only slightly higher: the median is $6,968 in smaller communities and $8,819 in cities of 250,000–500,000, and ranges from a low of $6,120 in the southern states to a high median of $8,772 in western states.[2]

The situation of the police officer is much like that of the extraordinary administrative secretary. The compensation in no way reflects the responsibility of either occupation. It is easy to understand why many officers need to moonlight in order to have the kind of living standard that they want for their wives and themselves. However, special problems for their wives may arise. How about social planning or even planning for meals? How much time does the officer get to spend with his children as head of the family? The combination of not being able to bring his work home with him and share it with his wife and having very little time at home anyway presents a most difficult problem with which the officer must cope.

It must be further recognized that the police officer has the same kinds of personal problems as everyone else. Unfortunately, again, the general public is too unaware of this element.

CONSTANT EXPOSURE TO
PERSONAL DANGER

Violence is a potential in any police action. When called, the officer may have little or no idea what he will find—or whether this will be his last assignment. Although in reality statistics do not support the melodrama that one views on the screen, the psychological impact of the job cannot adequately be measured. And the element of real danger to the officer is not less. An officer never knows whether the person he stops for a traffic violation is just a careless citizen or an armed criminal. Increasing numbers of policemen have been killed while attending to what normally would be a routine traffic violation. The increased use of drugs and alcohol is one reason, but knowing the possible cause in no way lessens the danger that rides with the law enforcement officer.

> The police officer is the only criminal justice professional who regularly sees the *victim* and *the damage the criminal act has caused.* The police officer talks to the molested child, sees the results of a brutal beating, views the bloody dead body of the filling station operator who has been ruthlessly and unnecessarily killed by the robber. He must identify the young girl killed or mutilated by a drunken driver, and notify her parents. He listens to the heroin addict pleading for a "fix," and tries to comfort the old couple defrauded of their life savings. No other person, in the criminal justice system comes into such constant direct contact with the victim. Actually, few of the professionals in the criminal system ever see the victim. . . . No matter how professional he is, the policeman who has walked on the bloody scene gets his mind "inflamed," and finds it hard to forget what he saw when he faces the offender.[3]

Neither the written word nor the action captured on film can reveal all of the emotional impact that is part of law enforcement. One may flinch or turn his head away as he views an officer helping to remove a badly burned, mutilated, or charred body from a wrecked automobile. The officer has no such option. He must even endure the stench and actual feel of the victim's body. As one officer put it, "We worked for over an hour to free the charred remains of a body from that burned truck. When I got home what do you think my wife had for dinner—barbecue."

If it is reported that the average patrolman's work is more tedious than dangerous, more monotonous than glamorous, it must be remembered that the relatively few policemen assigned to special details may have more exciting beats but they also have more tension. These men generally are on high risk assignments in areas of high crime. They must be constantly vigilant during their entire eight-hour shift, for at any moment they may become the victims of some drug-crazed individual or get killed in some gun battle with armed robbers. More tension-producing may be the bomb threats that must be investigated. The quiet nights can be worse than the busy ones for, over time, the anxiety of waiting can be maddening and "by 2 A.M. these men could more easily be shot from a cannon than put to bed."[4]

It is no wonder that many police officers who draw such assignments wind up in bars frequented by police, where they talk about dramatic incidents of their shifts that did or did not happen. Obviously most of this behavior is tension-reducing behavior. It is socially acceptable if not satisfactory. One would be hard put to say that socially acceptable means of relieving such tension should not be available to police officers. They might well need much more than an opportunity to talk or strut or brag to wipe away all that they had seen or experienced during a particular shift. Yet few departments afford the relaxing and reassuring help that would be most meaningful to men who legitimately need it so much.

THE POLICEMAN AS A HUMAN

Like many Americans, the policeman is at once an individual and a member of a minority group. Just as other minority citizens comprise a visible collective because of their color or speech, the officer is visible because of his uniform. Perhaps social scientists, politicians, and the rest of us do no more disservice to a minority individual—racial, ethnic, professional—than to judge him as a member of a group and to draw neat conclusions about the individual from what we know or assume of the class.

Conscientious policemen can have their respectability compromised by the generally deplored actions of an officer abusing his authority. Likewise, the bigot or incompetent can cloak his deeds in the professionalism of his fellows. Judgments passed upon policemen as a class make the individual officer's job more difficult. It is unfortunately true that some of our law enforcement agencies are rife with bigotry and corruption. It is also true that some of our most professional and compassionate people are members of police departments.

The chief of police must hold himself personally accountable for the unprofessional officers in his department. It is regrettable that when confronted with the behavior of an obviously racist or brutal officer too many chiefs of police will protect him. Frequently the response is, "He's a good cop. Maybe he does overreact a little sometimes. But he is a good policeman." When citizens accept that excuse and permit that officer to remain on the force, they are only inviting more violent conduct, and that, in turn, hurts the entire department and does damage to recruiting efforts.

For example, graduates of a behavioral science institute designed to produce a high-level trainee for potential police duty

were interviewed about their employment plans. Of the total gradu-
ating class only one would consider employment by a large metropolitan force in a prominent Texas city. While that particular department has some dedicated and exceptional officers, its condoning
of police excesses has almost destroyed a potentially excellent
source of recruits. The citizenry of that city, as well as the policemen themselves and their officials who admit the abusive conduct,
are responsible for the situation. The city is desperately undermanned and will continue to be undermanned until the overall
climate has changed. If community support had been placed with
the better officers, and if high-level officials had rid the department
of undesirables, that particular city would have no problem recruiting from all segments of the society, and particularly the minority
group segment.

The tendency to support departments and not police officers
must change. Support and reward must go to the officers who
deport themselves as professionals regardless of any other factors.
It is essential to stoutly condemn and take action against the unprofessional policeman. Of course the accused officer should have his
day in court, but if he is found guilty, appropriate action should
be taken.

Police want and need concern, respect, and even affection.
Like any other individual, the officer responds to humane treatment
and acceptance as a human being. If it looks as though London
or other European cities have the kind of law enforcement that
we prefer, our attitude must change and we must heavily reward
professional behavior and exemplary police-community conduct,
not only of patrolmen but also of chiefs of police. When the chief
of police cannot function in a manner that gets respect and obedi-
ence from his men in the area of their human relations conduct,
he ought to be removed.

In too many instances incompetent men are promoted. The
chief is made a director of public safety rather than being retired,
so that the effective workings of the police department will not
be compromised. If the retirement system for the police officer
is inadequate and might work a hardship on the chief of police,
something needs to be done about the retirement system. At any
rate, incompetence must not be allowed in a job as important as
that of chief of police.

Given the essentially political nature of police work, given
the controversial nature of some of the issues with which an officer
deals, and given our tendency to judge individuals on what we
know of their group, the policeman can find himself in an all but
impossible situation. Support for the men who are charged to pro-

tect us is mandatory. Only if it is made clear that we will support none but the highly professional, humane, well-trained officer will police departments come to understand that the general public has a right to police professionalism.

However, mere verbalization will not help. The general public must be apprised of the problems facing the police officer. The general public must awaken to the fact that there will always be a one-to-one relationship between the kind of police officer who serves them and the kind of backing they give to the police function. A recent survey shows that minority groups, especially black groups, are organizing to support police departments. Started several years ago because of the professionalism of a few police officers and the appreciation it aroused in minority groups, this movement has continued quietly. "Support Your Local Police" must be in the hearts of all Americans and not in the hands of a questionable vested interest group.

CHAPTER 10

COOPERATIVE
CRIME PREVENTION:
A MODEL

Since the middle 1960s, there have been many police–community relations programs. They have differed in design, but the ultimate goal was to bring police and community closer together for purposes of mutual understanding. Among these programs were the Grand Rapids program, the Tampa White Hat Patrol, the PACE program, and, of course, the Houston Cooperative Crime Prevention Program that achieved national attention. No program was, or is, to be considered bad. Most programs, including the Houston one, were planned and carried out in a time of crisis. The major concern was to put out a fire. In most cases positive results were achieved; that is to say, the symptoms of some deep underlying problems were removed. But actually little or nothing was done to erase the cause. It is rather like giving an aspirin to relieve the pain of a headache without checking to see what might have caused that headache or, having determined the cause, doing nothing else. Consequently, one cannot say that the problem has been solved for it may be festering underneath an uneasy calm. This is the reason the present chapter was written.

It is imperative to think in terms of a *comprehensive crime prevention program* rather than of police–community relations programs. In their time, police–community relations programs served a specific purpose or attempted to meet a specific need. The early targets were minority groups, more especially the black community. Some youth groups and antiwar activists were included as target populations. Violent confrontations between police and these groups were studied and various techniques were employed in an effort to ameliorate the intense hostility that seemed to characterize all meetings between them.

Most of the programs reported extreme resistance on the part of most chiefs of police and most officers—particularly command officers. The rigid defensive stance assumed by the police made real communication almost impossible and prevented the kind of success generally achieved in similar situations with other groups. Law enforcement officers, being a closed society and in a power position, often proved to be an intimidating factor. Many civilian participants expressed fear of reprisal. On the other hand, some officers voiced concern about retaliation from their superiors should they deal honestly in the sessions and admit police misconduct. The whole atmosphere served to make most programs an exhausting and frustrating experience for group leaders and participants.

Despite the factors working against the goals of positive police–community relations, it is obvious that most programs were beneficial to the communities that instituted them. However, the problems that gave rise to these efforts are not the problems with which our society is faced now. Most of the distrust, hostility, and resentment against police by minority groups persists, but the rapid rise of crime rates overshadows the civil rights activities and antiwar demonstrations that earlier involved these individuals and law enforcement agents. Actually, the overall problem is much more complex.

Increased professionalism, better training, better pay, minority recruitment, minority advancement, and other reforms are slowly reducing the traditional negative attitudes of minorities against police. Nonetheless, much antipathy remains because harassment, undue use of force, and verbal abuse are still practiced by some officers. A rash of police murders, along with the uncovering of police corruption in several departments, has added to the difficulties faced by law enforcement agencies all over the country. Organized crime and a sharp rise in drug trafficking and drug-related criminal activities while forces are badly undermanned further complicate the picture. Clearly there is a need for close cooperation between communities and police if the upsurge of crime and the poor police image are to be successfully attacked.

Simple police–community relations programs are no longer enough. Likewise, more police equipment alone will not solve the problem. It is time to realize that police hardware and the use of sophisticated crime detection and prevention instruments will accomplish only a part of the job—and one might say only a *small* part of the job. Crimes are committed by humans, and humans are complex. If crime is to be prevented, the greatest impact will come through the efficient use of other humans rather than only the highly technical design of crime-fighting tools.

This is not to say that human resources have been used inefficiently. But they have been used in a very limited way. First, it must be admitted that a small percentage of time is allotted to human relations training in the overall programs of police academies. Many academies have no programs, and others offer as few as six hours of training in human relations. Much of the human relations training is in reality "public relations" training and is devoid of the accurate history of past and present inhuman, discriminatory practices within the system.

Second, use of outside behavioral scientists or their techniques that might find positive application in police practice is inexcusably limited. Of course, there are behavioral scientists who lack sufficient training, experience, or understanding of police-community problems, but over the years since the middle 1960s much experience and expertise has been gained.

Since crime is a social problem, fighting it effectively will mean working through social institutions comprised of all kinds of people. In other words, the prevention of crime cannot be left totally to law enforcement. It demands a cooperative endeavor between the law enforcement officer and other members and agencies of the larger society. A major problem has been getting the kind of cooperation necessary to assist the police officer, who has the primary responsibility for the prevention of crime, as well as detection and apprehension.

There are many reasons for this reluctance to cooperate. In the past the public was satisfied to blame minority groups, liberals, so-called left-wingers, so-called Communists, and anyone else who dared criticize the current methods of carrying out the law enforcement function, or the government function. This was no solution, any more than continuous efforts geared to *doing the same thing* were a solution. Attempts to rid the nation of these so-called anti-law-enforcement groups by harassment, jailing, and other kinds of punishment have been unavailing.

Just as rhetoric failed to solve the problem, so this kind of reactive behavior failed to make a dent in it. It is time for both sides to stop playing defense. Scores are seldom made this way. It is time for both sides to stop blaming each other. Solutions to problems are not found this way. Certainly there must be means by which rationality can make inroads into highly irrational thinking and highly emotional behavior growing out of reaction-type situations.

The program that will be described addresses the complexity, the insidious elements, and the complications that arise when one tries to develop a truly comprehensive crime prevention program in the area of human behavior change. The program takes into consideration many of the indirect and oblique kinds of situations that have a direct impact upon law enforcement officers in their role of dealing with crime. As an example, a chief of police told an officer never to bring his personal problems to him or to the department. He said, "When you come here, leave your personal problems at home. When you are here, you are a police officer and I expect you to behave like one." Is it possible that this chief of police expected his words to wash away the frustration and the pain being experienced by the officer? Did the chief really expect the man to function at maximum efficiency by virtue of his giving of a directive?

We tend either to forget or to dismiss the fact that the same things that affect us as humans will affect the law enforcement officer as a human. It is time to acknowledge this fact and start dealing with law enforcement personnel both as trained, efficient professionals and as human beings. The two are not incongruent.

The Comprehensive Crime Prevention Program has two major thrusts: (1) education and training of the community and (2) consideration of the total life-space of the individual law enforcement person.

In the past both human relations and public relations aspects of the law enforcement function have been most inefficient. Police officers who have been delegated these functions are usually poorly equipped either in terms of training and background or in terms of manpower. In addition, too many law enforcement agencies view such projects as social work and ridicule those men who attempt to carry them out.

Some police departments are doing an excellent job in public relations but are failing in their efforts to improve human relations. On the other hand, many departments are doing a very poor job in human relations because they are unable to capture the imagination or the interest of the public, which they consider apathetic. The fact is, what they see as apathy is merely a symptom of extreme frustration on the part of the citizenry. It is a kind of giving up, a feeling of hopelessness and some impotent rage. The ultimate result is two very frustrated groups, both wanting to achieve the same end and neither being able to communicate with the other.

COMMUNITY EDUCATION AND TRAINING
Organizational Support

Every community is composed of a number of organizations, some having more strength and impact' upon the community than others. Regardless of the stature of these groups, their leaders should be brought together in a formal session guided by behavioral scientists and assisted by knowledgeable and "acceptable" law enforcement officers. The purpose of the meeting should be to make clear the degree, extent, and kinds of crime being committed in that particular community. In a very large city this project is carried on within police districts or using other kinds of boundary lines that are already established. After having been thoroughly briefed, the leaders should go back to their organizations and begin a series of public information programs that actually reach the people in the community.

In the past, even law-abiding citizens in minority communities viewed efforts of this nature with suspicion if attempted only by police. Few of them tried to take the message to the larger community because attitudes already formed and based on real, unfortunate experiences with some police would have rendered the effort useless. Enthusiastic reception of any program presented by law enforcement personnel does not mean that cooperation will be equally enthusiastic. There is too long a history of abuse and neglect on the part of too many police officers. A successful program must assure follow-up in the community in order to enhance and/or motivate *real* support at all levels. This can be accomplished in many ways, and each must be determined by the nature of the particular community.

Community Support

A second step in this phase of the program is threefold. It involves proper selection and special (additional) training of officers who will work in minority group areas. It demands as wide personal introduction as possible of these officers to individuals in their patrol area. The introductions should be handled relatively formally to community leaders and informally "on the beat." Finally, special small-group sessions describing the roles and heavy responsibilities of law enforcement persons should be directed in a manner that will give the participants much greater awareness than they have had in the past. Evaluations of all police–community relations programs have pointed to the high degree of relationship between improved police–community relations and awareness of police problems. When people really understand, they are much more "understanding."

Any program of crime prevention should begin with a well-informed (accepting) public whose information has been gained through programs designed for maximum effectiveness and impact. These programs must be able to deal with the suspicion, distrust, and other negative feelings that have sabotaged previous efforts at getting meaningful community support.

CONCERN FOR THE TOTAL LIFE-SPACE
OF THE LAW ENFORCEMENT PERSON
On-the-Job Problems

For the most part law enforcement is at least quasi-military. Consequently command officers often have unlimited authority, and the junior officer has little or no right of redress. In some situations junior officers dare not question the orders of their superiors. Sometimes junior officers will not talk freely in front of senior officers in even relatively innocuous circumstances. This is not a healthy atmosphere and can result in the junior officer's harboring a tremendous amount of hostility. Unexpressed, the hostility may manifest itself through unprofessional behavior toward an innocent citizen. Healthy lines of communication can be set up between senior and junior officers with no diminution of respect. Open communication is vitally important to good interpersonal relationships.

Numerous on-the-job problems are faced by police officers, but too often this military-type climate prevents their being aired. Although there are good reasons for a quasi-military organization, inflexibility or complete rigidity of thinking has no place in it. The problems faced by the officer may seem trivial or unimportant to his superior, but to that man or woman they may be unbearable and can adversely affect performance.

Sometimes complaints brought by citizens are placed in the offending officer's folder, and despite his being cleared he may not be informed of the action, or the complaint may continue as a part of his file. This true incident occurred during a training situation. It was amazing how morale went up when the supervisory personnel were instructed to notify an officer at once of the disposition of his case and to remove the file from his folder when there was no guilt.

Another example shows the resentment felt by officers who receive rewards for the number of traffic tickets issued but in some way are punished for not meeting a quota in a stipulated time span. These officers were not rewarded for crime prevention or everyday acts of good police–community relations. Police are indignant at not being able (in many cases) to make a ticket "stick" with the affluent while having an "easy" time with the economically disadvantaged citizen who may unconsciously break a law. The question of fair play haunts an officer who feels that he cannot afford to discuss it openly with his peers or his command officers.

If we are to have truly effective agencies, and officers who are functioning at an optimum level, one requisite is actual mutual respect and concern among the personnel. This cannot be accomplished in an atmosphere of resentment, distrust, or fear. Unfortunately, the negative attitudes are not always obvious, but left to fester they can become cancerous.

In-house discussions should be planned by professionals with the aim of eliminating or at least alleviating personnel problems that might adversely influence police behavior or departmental excellence.

Promotions, rules for writing tickets, civilian complaints, and other acts and rules that are internal must be considered in the light of their effect upon the law enforcement officer. Too often command officers fear warm personal relationships with their subordinates and are rigid and demanding; cooperation from them is grudging. Such behavior can lead to internal conflict, but the true cause of the conflict may not be admitted in an atmosphere of alienation.

Family

Programs of family group discussion of various problems, family opportunities for recreation, and counseling opportunities for families must be provided for officers. Most important is the counseling program for wives of police officers or for other members of the family. Too often the family does not really comprehend the nature of the policeman's work or the pressures to which he is constantly subjected. Or family members find no release for the anxieties created by their knowledge of the dangerous work he does. This area should be addressed by behavioral scientists or by law enforcement officers who are trained in counseling. No officer can function at optimum level if he is concerned about some family problem.

The Officer

There should be group or individual counseling for officers who find themselves in a state of anxiety or who have minor problems related to their jobs or to any phase of their lives. It is important that the police officer be mentally healthy. Since he does not work in a healthy atmosphere, there is no question about his being affected psychologically. This situation should be faced forthrightly, and he should be assisted to maintain his mental health in so unsavory a climate. The negative attitude toward means of maintaining mental health must be erased from the minds of command officers and the police themselves despite the fact that it remains in the minds of too many members of the general public. One does not have to be "crazy" to seek or make use of psychological counsel. The responsibilities of the police officer demand that he preserve his emotional maturity and his psychological balance.

A comprehensive program that allows the officer to know his public and the public to really know the officer creates the kind of climate that is conducive to improved functioning by both. The cooperative and even collaborative environment that results will facilitate the work of the police officer in crime deterrence, as well as in the apprehension of the criminal.

It is doubtful that any program will solve all of the problems of law enforcement. However, if as many relative elements as possible can be built into a program and it is designed for continuous follow-up and improvement, chances for success will be greatly enhanced. Cooperative endeavor built upon mutual trust and respect can not only ensure the safety of a community but improve the quality of life within it. Police are people. When police (who often are not seen as people) and "people" (citizens) realize this, their collaborative efforts may bring about "equal protection under the law" and "liberty and justice for all."

Group Activity

Most police–community relations programs unwittingly threw together individuals who disliked and distrusted one another. They came with their stereotyped biases and their best defenses. It was as if they came to do battle, rather than to develop lines of communication. Neither group (police or citizens) had a sufficient grasp of the problems and concerns of the other. In fact, neither really cared about the problems or concerns of the other. Each came to fight and to win.

Although such meetings can result in some catharsis, which may be helpful, it is usually a temporary defusing of a volatile situation. The elements for enduring respect and understanding growing out of mutual exchange seldom get an opportunity to emerge. Much of this stricture is due to the individual's problem with himself.

The recommended community and police preliminary sessions are geared to prepare for communication between the groups in an atmosphere of understanding and with a view to attacking a mutual problem—crime. Minorities suffer most from crime. They need the police and the police need them, because the total community is the ultimate one to suffer from unchecked criminal activity. The loss to the individual in goods and in taxes can be tremendous.

Small, volunteer group activity should follow the separate

preparation sessions. Discussions should be based on means of fighting burglary, rape, assault, drug trafficking, and the like, in the community. Each situation will differ, so no one solution will fit all cases. However, a spirit of cooperation in itself can do much to deter crime in that the criminal quickly learns that the chink in the armor of law enforcement (police–community hostility) has been closed and he is no longer free to continue his activity. Joint solutions to crime in the community mean more eyes, more information, confidence in law enforcement, and efforts toward mutual protection.

Small-group discussions and cooperative effort should be ongoing, the ultimate goal being the eradication of all crime in the community. This may be an impossible objective, but it is a worthy one and assures continuous collaboration between two groups that once thrived on mutual hate.

AFTERWORD:

TOWARD A SYSTEM
OF JUSTICE

The actual administration of justice requires much more than laws and an adversary system to assure that justice does in fact prevail. Laws are made and administered by humans and are subject to human frailty and human failure. Hence stringent safeguards must become a part of the fabric of our system of justice.

Especially must we be careful that they who develop our laws, they who interpret them, and they who administer them never place themselves above those laws.

We must be ever mindful that the have-nots and the have-littles of our country have a right to equal protection under the laws. Minority groups and the poor must be beneficiaries and not victims of our system of justice.

Adequate and proper law enforcement is a strong deterrent to crime, but law enforcement that is neither adequate nor proper can *breed* crime. Technical crime-fighting equipment is mandatory and has to receive attention. However, our major concern must be the *quality of criminal justice personnel*—judges, lawyers, police officers, jailers, guards, and others who are a part of the total system. Laws are no better than the individuals who are sworn to administer them impartially and without exception. This may mean a strong drive for the development and use of better screening devices for all criminal justice personnel.

Law is necessary and order is necessary, but that law and order must be tempered with justice and compassion. There is no implication of a "coddling" of the criminal. The idea is merely to guarantee these rights:

AMENDMENT IV. The right of the people to be secure in their persons, houses, papers, and effects, against unreasonable searches and seizures, shall not be violated, and no Warrants shall issue, but upon probable cause, supported by oath or affirmation, and particularly describing the place to be searched, and the persons or things to be seized.[1]

AMENDMENT V. No person shall be held to answer for a capital, or otherwise infamous crime, unless on a presentment or in-dictment of a Grand Jury, except in cases arising in the land or naval forces . . . nor shall any person be subject for the same offense to be twice put in jeopardy of life or limb, nor shall be compelled in any criminal case to be a witness against himself, nor be deprived of life, liberty, or property, without due process of law. . . .[2]

AMENDMENT VI. In all criminal prosecutions, the accused shall enjoy the right to a speedy and public trial, by an impartial jury of the State and district wherein the crime shall have been committed . . . and to be informed of the nature and cause of the accusation; to be confronted with the witnesses against him; to have compulsory process for obtaining wit-nesses in his favor, and to have the Assistance of Counsel for his defense.[3]

AMENDMENT VIII. Excessive bail shall not be required, nor excessive fines imposed, nor cruel and unusual punishments inflicted.[4]

AMENDMENT XIV. . . . No State shall make or enforce any law which shall abridge the privileges or immunities of citi-zens of the United States; nor shall any State deprive any person of life, liberty, or property, without due process of law; nor deny to any person within its jurisdiction the equal protection of the laws.[5]

In other words, to accomplish the administration of *justice*.

The preceding chapters have examined the salient features of our criminal justice system: the personnel and peculiar problems of the law enforcement agencies and the court system. The topics covered range from procedural inadequacies to human abuse, from police excess to police powerlessness. Unpleasant realities have been acknowledged, and potential solutions have been suggested.

Yet the very existence of a criminal justice system perhaps tells us more about ourselves than the data presented, the incidents related, the reforms posited. A system, whether harsh or lenient, whether favoring the rights of the individual or those of society, represents an attempt to make permanent what would otherwise be temporal. The stockpiling of records, the codification of laws, the institutionalization of life in the form of behavior norms and penalties for their violation are all founded on the desire for perpetuation, for a history.

It is perhaps impossible to understand the expectations or the stress of police work without understanding that its essential function is to preserve the status quo. A policeman's statutory duty is to enforce the law, whether he feels it to be right or wrong himself.

Kerper answers the question "What is law?" by stating that it is *one* means of social control.

> Law is distinguishable from all other means of social control because the reasons for decision, the place of decision, the rules which govern decision making, and the limits of the sanctions are set out in advance. The individual knows before he undertakes the alleged act where, how, by whom, and under what conditions he will be judged. He knows what conduct has been declared illegal, and the limits of the punishments he may suffer.[6]

Law is defined as

> . . . a formal means of social control that involves the use of rules that are interpreted and are enforceable by the courts of a political community.[7]

Our criminal justice system is designed to guarantee that an individual accused of breaking a rule (the law) has every opportunity to be heard through the court procedure. The criminal justice process in the United States of America is indeed complex, but that very complexity serves to safeguard the rights of the accused (or the defendant). For a number of reasons, explains Kerper, not all individuals go all the way through that system, but it is there to assure fair and impartial judgment. Basically, the machinery of the criminal justice process is geared for the individual and toward a constructive end: *the administration of justice*.

Like all other machinery created by man, it is vulnerable to breakdown, despite its power over the life or death of an individual. Like all inventors and operators we like to accent the positive and ignore the negative. However, unless along with accenting the positive we attend to the negative, the end result of our arduous and studied labor can be disastrous.

Minorities—and more particularly the blacks—in America have been victims rather than beneficiaries of the criminal justice system. Much the same can be said for the economically disadvantaged regardless of race or ethnicity. Were this disparity in treatment accidental, even though it fell to the lot of a certain segment of society, it might at least be understood if not tolerated. In too many instances, however, the injustice to the individual is deliberate. This cannot continue to be countenanced.

Currently, the police officer receives almost all the blame for the ills of our system of justice. There are many reasons for this state of affairs, but the blame is not his alone. The individual in society must assume his share of the responsibility, for much of the problem has grown out of his apathy and/or his ignorance.

It can only be hoped that the police officer (who normally pushes the button that starts the machinery), the counselors, judges, prison officials, bail bondsmen, jurors, and the many other persons whose function is to facilitate the judicial process will look again at how the system may *not* be working.

Our country was built on the principles of equality and justice. If that foundation is permitted to fail for a few, the many ultimately will be caught in a catastrophic aftermath. Attended to immediately and with true commitment, the weaknesses in our criminal justice process can be corrected. That done, *all* Americans can say with determination and a sense of national pride, "With liberty and *justice* for *all*."

NOTES

INTRODUCTION

1. Ardrienne Koch and William Peden, eds., *The Life and Selected Writings of Thomas Jefferson*, Modern Library, New York, 1944, p. 322.
2. Carl Sandburg, *Abraham Lincoln: The War Years*, vol. 1, Harcourt Brace Jovanovich, New York, 1939, p. 133.

CHAPTER 1

1. *Report of the National Advisory Commission on Civil Disorders*, Bantam, New York, 1968, p. 213.
2. Ibid., p. 218.
3. Ibid., p. 218.
4. Ibid., p. 116.
5. Shalom Endleman, ed., *Violence in the Streets*, Quadrangle, Chicago, 1968, p. 330.
6. Ibid.
7. Robert L. Allen, *Black Awakening in Capitalist America*, Anchor Books, Garden City, N.Y., 1969, p. 134.
8. Tom Hayden, *Rebellion in Newark: Official Violence and Ghetto Response*, Vintage Books, New York, 1967, p. 50.
9. Ibid., pp. 50–53.
10. Ibid., p. 53.
11. *Report of the National Advisory Commission*, op. cit., p. 206.
12. George Clifton Edwards, *Police on the Urban Frontier*, Institute of Human Relations Press, New York, 1968, p. 27, citing *Washington Post*, June 29, 1967.
13. A. J. Reiss, Jr., "Police Brutality—Answers to Key Questions," *Transaction*, vol. 5, July–August 1968, p. 16. Published by permission of Transaction, Inc. from *Society*. Copyright ©1968 by Transaction, Inc.
14. Arthur Niederhoffer, *Behind the Shield: The Police in Urban Society*, Anchor Books, Garden City, N.Y., 1967, p. 194, citing Stanley Lieberson and Arnold Silverman. Copyright ©1967 by Arthur Niederhoffer. Reprinted by permission of Doubleday & Co., Inc.
15. David H. Bayley and Harold Mendelsohn, *Minorities and the Police: Confrontation in America*, Free Press, New York, 1969, p. 107.
16. James Q. Wilson, *Varieties of Police Behavior: The Management of Law and Order in Eight Communities*, Harvard University Press, Cambridge, Mass., 1968, p. 43.
17. Jerome H. Skolnick, *The Politics of Protest: Violent Aspects of Protest and Confrontation*, U.S. Government Printing Office, Washington, D.C., 1969, p. 183, citing James Baldwin.
18. *Mexican-Americans and the Administration of Justice in the Southwest*, U.S. Government Printing Office, Washington, D.C., March 1970, p. 12, citing *Task Force Report: The Police*.
19. "Guest Viewpoint," *Daily Texan*, Austin, Texas, November 17, 1973.
20. *Task Force Report: The Police*, U.S. Government Printing Office, Washington, D.C., 1967, p. 148, citing John F. Kraft, Inc., "Attitudes of Negroes in Various Cities."
21. Ibid., citing Raymond Galvin and Louis Radelet.
22. "Bias in the Jury Box," *Time*, vol. 95, April 6, 1970, p. 61.
23. "Situation Report," *Time*, vol. 95, April 6, 1970, p. 61.
24. *Report of the National Advisory Commission*, op. cit., p. 268.

25. *Report of the Task Force on Human Rights,* National Education Association, Washington, D.C., 1968, p. 20.
26. Niederhoffer, op. cit., p. 12, quoting Dan Dodson.
27. *Mexican-Americans,* op. cit., p. 12, citing Western Center Study.
28. Douglas Ross, *Robert K. Kennedy: Apostle of Change,* Pocket Books, New York, 1968, p. 140.
29. *Report of the Task Force,* op. cit., p. 22.
30. Arnold Rose, *The Negro in America,* Harper & Row, New York, 1948, pp. 176–177.
31. Ibid., p. 177.
32. Reiss, op. cit., pp. 13–14.
33. Ibid., p. 15.
34. Ibid., p. 12.
35. Ibid.
36. Ibid., pp. 12–13.
37. Ibid., p. 13.
38. Ibid., p. 14.
39. Ibid., p. 18.
40. Johnny Spain, "The Black Family and the Prisons," *Black Scholar,* vol. 4, October 1972, p. 25.
41. Phillip G. Zimbardo, "Pathology of Imprisonment," *Society,* vol. 9, April 1972, p. 8.
42. Jessica Mitford, "Experiments Behind Bars," *Atlantic Monthly,* vol. 231, January 1973, pp. 64–65. Copyright ©1972, by The Atlantic Monthly Company, Boston, Mass. Reprinted with permission.

CHAPTER 2

1. Abe Fortas, *Concerning Dissent and Civil Disobedience,* New American Library, New York, 1968, p. 33.
2. *Mexican-Americans and the Administration of Justice in the Southwest,* U.S. Government Printing Office, Washington, D.C., March 1970, p. 31.
3. George Clifton Edwards, *Police on the Urban Frontier,* Institute of Human Relations Press, New York, 1968, p. 73.
4. *Task Force Report: The Police,* U.S. Government Printing Office, Washington, D.C., 1967, p. 195, citing National Capital Area Civil Liberties Union, "A Proposed Revision of the System for Processing Complaints Against Police Misconduct in the District of Columbia, January 1964."
5. Ibid., p. 203, citing Samuel Greason.

CHAPTER 3

1. Nicholas Alex, *Black in Blue,* Appleton, New York, 1969, pp. 13–14.
2. *Task Force Report: The Police,* U.S. Government Printing Office, Washington, D.C., 1967, p. 167.
3. Ibid., p. 169.
4. Ibid., p. 171.
5. Ibid.
6. *Mexican-Americans and the Administration of Justice in the Southwest,* U.S. Government Printing Office, Washington, D.C., March, 1970, p. 78.
7. Ibid.
8. Alex, op. cit., p. 139.
9. Ibid., p. 161.
10. *Task Force Report,* op. cit., p. 170, citing New York State Department of Labor.
11. A. J. Reiss, Jr., "Police Brutality—Answers to Key Questions," *Transaction,* vol. 5, July–August 1968, p. 16. Published by permission of Transaction, Inc. from *Society.* Copyright © 1968 by Transaction, Inc.
12. Alex, op. cit., p. xvi.

PART TWO
1. Bruce Wasserstein and Mark J. Green, eds., *With Justice for Some: An Indictment of the Law by Young Advocates*, Beacon, Boston, 1970, p. 193. Copyright © 1970 by Bruce Wasserstein and Mark J. Green. Reprinted by permission of Beacon press.
2. *Texas New Release*, Austin, Texas, March 15, 1974.

CHAPTER 4
1. Harry W. Jones, ed., *The Courts, the Public, and the Law Explosion*, Prentice-Hall, Englewood Cliffs, N.J., 1965, p. 9.
2. Bruce Wasserstein and Mark J. Green, eds., *With Justice for Some*, Beacon, Boston, 1970, pp. ix–x, Introduction by Ralph Nader. Copyright © 1970 by Bruce Wasserstein and Mark J. Green. Reprinted by permission of Beacon Press.
3. Howard James, *Crisis in the Courts*, McKay, New York, 1971, p. vi, quoting Chief Justice Burger. Copyright © 1968 by the Christian Science Publishing Society. *From Crisis in the Courts* by Howard James. Published by David McKay Company, Inc. Reprinted with permission of the publishers.
4. Wasserstein and Green, op. cit., p. 193.
5. Jones, op. cit., p. 2.
6. James, op. cit., p. v, quoting Chief Justice Burger.
7. Charles A. Reich, "The New Property," Yale Law Journal, vol. 73, April 1964, p. 738. Reprinted by permission of The Yale Law Journal Company and Fred B. Rothman & Company.
8. Ibid., p. 739.
9. Ibid., p. 746.
10. *Court Reform: Key to a Balanced Criminal Justice System*, Advisory Commission on Intergovernmental Relations, Washington, D.C., 1971, p. 1.
11. James, op. cit., p. iv, quoting Chief Justice Burger.
12. Ibid., p. vi.
13. Ibid., pp. 37–38.
14. Ibid., p. xii, quoting Chief Justice Burger.
15. Ibid., p. 4.
16. Ibid.
17. *Court Reform*, op. cit., p. 3.
18. Josiah G. Holland, "God Give Us Men," *Treasury of the Familiar*, Ralph I. Woods, eds., vol. 1, Macmillan Publishing Company, Riverside, N.J., 1942, p. 34.
19. Jay Schulman et al. "Recipe for a Jury," *Psychology Today*, vol. 6, May 1973, p. 41. Reprinted from *Psychology Today* Magazine. Copyright © Ziff-Davis Publishing Company.
20. Wasserstein and Green, op. cit., pp. 193–194.
21. James, op. cit., pp. 82–83.
22. Ibid., p. 11.
23. *Court Reform*, op. cit., p. 2.
24. Ibid., p. 3.
25. James, op. cit., p. 10.
26. *Court Reform*, op. cit., p. 3.
27. Wasserstein and Green, op. cit., p. 194.

CHAPTER 5
1. Hazel B. Kerper, *Introduction to the Criminal Justice System*, West, St. Paul, Minn., 1972, p. 291.
2. Louis L. Knowles and Kenneth Prewitt, eds., *Institutional Racism in America*, Prentice-Hall, Englewood Cliffs, N.J., 1969, p. 73.
3. Ibid., p. 74, citing Patricia Wald.
4. Ibid., p. 74.

5. Ibid.
6. Ibid., p. 73.
7. Ibid.
8. *Mexican-Americans and the Administration of Justice in the Southwest*, U.S. Government Printing Office, Washington, D.C., March, 1970, p. x, citing U.S. Department of Agriculture, Agricultural Economic Report No. 112.
9. Ibid., p. 58.
10. *Better Prosecution and Defense Vital to Justice*, Advisory Commission on Intergovernmental Relations, Washington, D.C., 1972, p. 4.
11. "Bias in the Jury Box," *Time*, vol. 95, April 6, 1970, p. 61.
12. Ibid.
13. Charles E. Goodell, "Where Did the Grand Jury Go?" *Harper's Magazine*, vol. 246, May 1973, pp. 14, 16. Used by permission of Random House, Inc. from *Political Prisoners in America*. Copyright ©1973 by Charles Goodell.
14. Ibid., p. 22.
15. *Hearing Before the United States Commission on Civil Rights*, U.S. Governmental Printing Office, Washington, D.C., 1969, p. 668.

CHAPTER 6
1. "Situation Report," *Time*, Vol. 95, April 6, 1970, p. 61.
2. Louis L. Knowles and Kenneth Prewitt, eds., *Institutional Racism in America*, Prentice-Hall, Englewood Cliffs, N.J., 1969, pp. 66–67, quoting Anthony Lester.
3. Muhammad Ahmad, "We Are All Prisoners of War," *Black Scholar*, vol. 4, October 1972, p. 3.
4. Hazel B. Kerper, *Introduction to the Criminal Justice System*, West, St. Paul, Minn., 1972, p. 327.
5. Ibid., p. 337.
6. Knowles and Prewitt, op. cit., p. 68, citing U.S. Commission on Civil Rights, *Law Enforcement*.
7. "Episodes from the Attica Massacre," *Black Scholar*, vol. 4, October 1972, pp. 35–39. Reprinted with permission.
8. *Mexican-Americans and the Administration of Justice*, U.S. Government Printing Office, Washington, D.C., March 1970, p. 48, citing Federal Rules of Criminal Procedure.
9. Monrad G. Paulsen and Sanford H. Kadish, *Criminal Law and Its Processes*, Little, Brown and Co., Boston, 1962, pp. 931–932.
10. Ibid., p. 931.
11. Knowles and Prewitt, op. cit., p. 72.
12. Paulsen and Kadish, op. cit., p. 931.
13. Knowles and Prewitt, op. cit., p. 73, citing Daniel J. Freed and Patricia M. Wald.
14. Howard James, *Crisis in the Courts*, McKay, New York, 1971, p. 114.
15. Mexican-Americans, op. cit., p. 50, citing interviews with Henry Trujillo, Samuel Willis, Jerry Thomas, chief, and Richard Walker, patrolman.
16. *Mecklenburg County Pre-Trial Release Program*, Mecklenburg County Pre-Trial Release Program, Charlotte, N.C., n.d.
17. *Community Based Corrections in Des Moines*, U.S. Department of Justice, Washington, D.C., pp. 12–13.

PART THREE
1. Douglas Ross, *Robert F. Kennedy: Apostle of Change*, Pocket Books, New York, 1968, p. 94.
2. Ibid., p. 96.
3. A. K. Brandstatter and Louis A. Radelet, eds., *Police and Community Relations: A Sourcebook*, Charles C Thomas, Springfield, Ill., 1968, p. 460.

4. Arthur Niederhoffer, Behind the Shield: *The Police in Urban Society,* Anchor Books, Garden City, N.Y., 1967, p. 1. Copyright © 1967 by Arthur Neiderhoffer. Reprinted by permission of Doubleday & Co., Inc.
5. Brandstatter and Radelet, op. cit., p. 460.
6. Ross, op. cit., p. 591.

CHAPTER 7
1. Harlan Hahn, ed., *Police in Urban Society,* Sage Publications, Beverly Hills, Calif., 1971, p. 293.
2. Thorsten Sellin, ed., *New Goals in Police Management,* American Academy of Political and Social Science, Philadelphia, January 1954, p. 6, citing William Parker.
3. Roy Fairfield, ed., *The Federalist Papers,* Anchor Books, Garden City, N.Y., 1966, p. 77.
4. James Q. Wilson, *Varieties of Police Behavior,* Harvard University Press, Cambridge, Mass., 1968, p. 84.
5. David H. Bayley and Harold Mendelsohn, *Minorities and the Police,* Free Press, New York, 1969, p. 19.
6. Seymour Martin Lipset, "Why Cops Hate Liberals—and Vice Versa," *Atlantic Monthly,* vol. 223, March 1969, p. 76. Copyright © 1969, by The Atlantic Monthly Company, Boston, Mass. Reprinted with permission.
7. Bayley and Mendelsohn, op. cit., pp. 19–20.
8. Niederhoffer, *Behind the Shield: The Police in Urban Society,* Anchor Books, Garden City, N.Y., 1967, p. 117. Copyright © 1967 by Arthur Neiderhoffer. Reprinted by permission of Doubleday & Co., Inc.
9. Lipset, op. cit., p. 76.
10. Ibid., p. 77.
11. William O. Douglas, *The Rights of Rebellion,* Vintage Books, New York, 1970, p. 58.
12. Hahn, op. cit., p. 293.
13. *Modernizing the Police—The Men in the Middle,* Advisory Commission on Intergovernmental Relations, Washington, D.C., 1971, p. 1.

CHAPTER 8
1. Hazel B. Kerper, *Introduction to the Criminal Justice System,* West, St. Paul, Minn., 1972, Garden City, N.Y.; 1967, Anchor Books, p. 417.
2. Ibid.
3. Ibid.
4. Arthur Niederhoffer, *Behind the Shield: The Police in Urban Society,* p. 38, citing respectively Leo Eilbert and others, Paul Bohardt, David Wilson, and Donald McDonald. Copyright © 1967 by Arthur Niederhoffer. Reprinted by permission of Doubleday & Co., Inc.
5. Seymour Martin Lipset, "Why Cops Hate Liberals—and Vice Versa," *Atlantic Monthly,* vol. 223, March 1969, p. 78, quoting Gunnar Myrdal. Copyright © 1969, by The Atlantic Monthly Company, Boston, Mass. Reprinted with permission.
6. Niederhoffer, op. cit., p. 41.
7. David H. Bayley and Harold Mendelsohn, *Minorities and the Police,* Free Press, New York, 1969, p. 3.
8. Charles B. Saunders, Jr., *Upgrading the American Police,* Brookings, Washington, D.C., 1970, p. 118.
9. Jerome H. Skolnick, *Justice Without Trial,* Wiley, New York, 1966, pp. 4–5.
10. Saunders, op. cit., p. 35.
11. Niederhoffer, op. cit., p. 139.
12. Thomas F. Adams, *Law Enforcement: An Introduction to the Police Role in the Community,* Prentice-Hall, Englewood Cliffs, N.J., 1968, pp. 216–217.

13. Niederhoffer, op. cit., pp. 25–26.
14. Kerper, op. cit., pp. 423–424.
15. James Q. Wilson, *Varieties of Police Behavior,* Harvard University Press, Cambridge, Mass., 1968, p. 85.
16. Gordon E. Misner, "Enforcement: Illusion of Security," *Nation,* vol. 208, April 21, 1969, p. 488.
17. Wilson, op. cit., p. 4, citing the President's Commission on Law Enforcement and the Administration of Justice.
18. Ibid., p. 6, citing the 1965 FBI Uniform Crime Reports.
19. Bayley and Mendelsohn, op. cit., p. 69.
20. James Q. Wilson, "What Makes a Better Policeman?" *Atlantic Monthly,* vol. 223, March 1969, p. 131.
21. Bayley and Mendelsohn, op. cit., p. 77, citing *The Challenge of Crime in a Free Society.*
22. *Modernizing the Police—The Men in the Middle,* Advisory Commission on Intergovernmental Relations, Washington, D.C., 1971, p. 2.
23. Urban America, Inc., Urban Coalition, *One Year Later,* Praeger, New York, 1969, p. 118.

CHAPTER 9
1. Gail Sheehy, "The Lonely Fear of a Policeman's Wife," *McCalls Magazine,* vol. 98, March 1971, p. 99.
2. Charles B. Saunders, Jr., *Upgrading the American Police,* Brookings, Washington, D.C., 1970, pp. 59–60, citing *The Municipal Yearbook.*
3. Hazel B. Kerper, *Introduction to the Criminal Justice System,* West, St. Paul, Minn., 1972, p. 427.
4. Sheehy, op. cit., pp. 96.

AFTERWORD
1. Sidney H. Asch, *Police Authority and the Rights of the Individual,* Arco, New York, 1967, p. 38.
2. Ibid., pp. 38–39.
3. Ibid., p. 39.
4. Ibid.
5. Ibid.
6. Hazel B. Kerper, *Introduction to the Criminal Justice System,* West, St. Paul, Minn., 1972, p. 7.
7. Ibid., p. 8, quoting Davis et al.

BIBLIOGRAPHY

Adams, Thomas F., *Law Enforcement: An Introduction to the Police Role in the Community*, Prentice-Hall, Englewood Cliffs, N.J., 1968.

Agnew, Spiro, "NSA Conference Address," *The National Sheriff*, August–September 1970.

Ahmad, Muhammad, "We Are All Prisoners of War," *The Black Scholar*, vol. 4, October 1972.

Alex, Nicholas, *Black in Blue*, Appleton, New York, 1969.

Allen, Robert L., *Black Awakening in Capitalist America*, Anchor Books, Garden City, N.Y., 1969.

Asch, Sidney H., *Police Authority and the Rights of the Individual*, Arco, New York, 1967.

Bayley, David H., and Harold Mendelsohn, *Minorities and the Police: Confrontation in America*, Free Press, New York, 1969.

Bennett, Lerone, Jr., *Before the Mayflower: A History of Black America*, Johnson Publishing Co., Chicago, 1969.

Better Prosecution and Defense Vital to Justice, Advisory Commission on Intergovernmental Relations, Washington, D.C., 1972.

"Bias in the Jury Box," *Time*, vol. 95, April 6, 1970.

Bordua, David J., ed., *The Police: Six Sociological Essays*, Wiley, New York, 1967.

Brandstatter, A. F., and Louis A. Radelet, eds., *Police and Community Relations: A Sourcebook*, Charles C Thomas, Springfield, Ill., 1968.

Community Based Corrections in Des Moines, U.S. Department of Justice, Washington, D.C., n.d.

Court Reform: Key to a Balanced Criminal Justice System, Advisory Commission on Intergovernmental Relations, Washington, D.C., 1971.

Douglas, William O., *The Rights of Rebellion*, Vintage Books, New York, 1970.

Edwards, George Clifton, *Police on the Urban Frontier*, Institute of Human Relations Press, New York, 1968.

Endleman, Shalom, ed., *Violence in the Streets*, Quadrangle, Chicago, 1968.

"Episodes from the Attica Massacre," *The Black Scholar*, vol. 4, October 1972.

Fairfield, Roy, ed., *The Federalist Papers*, Anchor Books, Garden City, N.Y., 1966.

Fortas, Abe, *Concerning Dissent and Civil Disobedience*, New American Library, New York, 1968.

Goodell, Charles E., "Where Did the Grand Jury Go?" *Harper's Magazine*, vol. 246, May 1973.

"Guest Viewpoint," *The Daily Texan*, Austin, Texas, November 17, 1973.

Hahn, Harlan, ed., *Police in Urban Society*, Sage Publications, Beverly Hills, Calif., 1971.

Hayden, Tom, *Rebellion in Newark: Official Violence and Ghetto Response*, Vintage Books, New York, 1967.

Hearing Before the United States Commission on Civil Rights, U.S. Government Printing Office, Washington, D.C. 1969.

James, Howard, *Crisis in the Courts,* McKay, New York, 1971.

Jones, Harry W., ed., *The Courts, the Public, and the Law Explosion,* Prentice-Hall, Englewood Cliffs, N.J., 1965.

Kerper, Hazel B., *Introduction to the Criminal Justice System,* West, St. Paul, Minn., 1972.

Knowles, Louis L., and Kenneth Prewitt, eds., *Institutional Racism in America,* Prentice-Hall, Englewood Cliffs, N.J., 1969.

Koch, Ardrienne, and William Peden, eds., *The Life and Selected Writings of Thomas Jefferson,* Modern Library, New York, 1944.

Lipset, Seymour Martin, "Why Cops Hate Liberals—and Vice Versa," *Atlantic Monthly,* vol. 223, March 1969.

Mecklenburg County Pre-Trial Release Program, Mecklenburg County Pre-Trial Release Program, Charlotte, N.C., n.d.

Mexican-Americans and the Administration of Justice in the Southwest, U.S. Government Printing Office, Washington, D.C., March 1970.

Misner, Gordon E., "Enforcement: Illusion of Security, "*The Nation,* vol. 208, April 21, 1969.

Mitford, Jessica, "Experiments Behind Bars," *Atlantic Monthly,* vol. 231, January 1973.

Modernizing the Police—The Men in the Middle, Advisory Commission on Intergovernmental Relations, Washington, D.C., 1971.

Niederhoffer, Arthur, *Behind the Shield: The Police in Urban Society,* Anchor Books, Garden City, N.Y., 1967.

Paulsen, Monrad G. and Sanford H. Kadish, *Criminal Law and Its Processes,* Little, Brown and Co., Boston, 1962.

Reich, Charles A., "The New Property," *Yale Law Journal,* vol. 73, April 1964.

Reiss, A. J., Jr., "Police Brutality: Answers to Key Questions," *Transaction,* vol. 5, July–August 1968.

Report of the National Advisory Commission on Civil Disorders, Bantam, New York, 1968.

Report of the Task Force on Human Rights, National Education Association, Washington, D.C., 1968.

Rose, Arnold, *The Negro in America,* Beacon, Boston, 1948.

Ross, Douglas, *Robert F. Kennedy: Apostle of Change,* Pocket Books, New York, 1968.

Sandburg, Carl, *Abraham Lincoln: The War Years,* vol. 1, Harcourt Brace Jovanovich, New York, 1939.

Saunders, Charles B., Jr., *Upgrading the American Police,* Brookings, Washington, D.C., 1970.

Schulman, Jay, and others, "Recipe for a Jury," *Psychology Today,* vol. 6, May 1973.

Sellin, Thorsten, ed., *New Goals in Police Management,* American Academy of Political and Social Science, Philadelphia, Pa., January 1954.

Sheehy, Gail, "The Lonely Fear of a Policeman's Wife," *McCalls Magazine,* vol. 98, March 1971.

"Situation Report," *Time,* vol. 95, April 6, 1970

Skolnick, Jerome H., *Justice Without Trial*, Wiley, New York, 1966.

Skolnick, Jerome H., *The Politics of Protest: Violent Aspects of Protest and Confrontation*, U.S. Government Printing Office, Washington, D.C., 1969.

Spain, Johnny, "The Black Family and the Prisons," *The Black Scholar*, vol. 4, October 1972.

Task Force Report: The Police, U.S. Government Printing Office, Washington, D.C., 1967.

Texas News Release, Austin, Texas, March 15, 1974.

Thorpe, Frances Newton, ed., *The Federal and State Constitutions*, Vol. I, U.S. Government Printing Office, Washington, D.C., 1909.

Urban America, Inc., *Urban Coalition, One Year Later*, Praeger, New York, 1969.

Venezia, Peter S., and Roger Steggerda, *Pre-Trial Release, Pre-Trial Release with Supportive Services, Residential Corrections*, National Council on Crime and Delinquency, Des Moines, Iowa, July 1973.

Wasserstein, Bruce, and Mark J. Green, eds., *With Justice for Some: An Indictment of the Law by Young Advocates*, Beacon, Boston, 1970.

"We Found Corruption to Be Widespread," Knapp Commission Report on New York Police, *U.S. News and World Report*, vol. 74, January 29, 1973.

Wilson, James Q., *Varieties of Police Behavior: The Management of Law and Order in Eight Communities*, Harvard University Press, Cambridge, Mass., 1968.

Wilson, James Q., "What Makes a Better Policeman?" *Atlantic Monthly*, vol. 223, March 1969.

Woods, Ralph I., ed., *Treasury of the Familiar*, vol. 1, Spencer Press, Chicago, 1942.

Zimbardo, Phillip G., "Pathology of Imprisonment," *Society*, vol. 9, April 1972.

INDEX

75 76 77 7 6 5 4 3 2 1